The IQ Workout Series

THE COMPLETE
BOOK OF
FUN MATHS

250 confidence-boosting tricks, tests and puzzles

Philip Carter and Ken Russell

WILEY

Published by John Wiley & Sons Ltd, The Atrium, Southern Gate, Chichester, West Sussex
PO19 8SQ, England

Telephone: (+44) 1243 779777
Email (for orders and customer service enquiries): cs-books@wiley.co.uk
Visit our Home Page on www.wileyeurope.com or www.wiley.com

Other Wiley Editorial Offices

John Wiley & Sons Inc., 111 River Street, Hoboken, NJ 07030, USA

Jossey-Bass, 989 Market Street, San Francisco, CA 94103-1741, USA

Wiley-VCH Verlag GmbH, Boschstrasse 12, D-69469 Weinheim, Germany

John Wiley & Sons Australia Ltd, 33 Park Road, Milton, Queensland 4064, Australia

John Wiley and Sons (Asia) Pte Ltd, 2 Clementi Loop #02–01, Jin Xing Distripark,
Singapore 129809

John Wiley & Sons Canada Ltd, 22 Worcester Road, Etobicoke, Ontario, Canada M9W 1L1

British Library Cataloguing in Publication Data

A catalogue record for this book is available from the British Library

ISBN 10: 0-470-87091-5 (PB) ISBN 13: 978-0-470-87091-4 (PB)

Typeset in 11/14 pt Garamond by Mathematical Composition Setters Ltd, Salisbury, Wiltshire.
Printed and bound in Great Britain by T. J. International Ltd, Padstow, Cornwall.
This book is printed on acid-free paper responsibly manufactured from sustainable forestry, in
which at least two trees are planted for each one used for paper production.

Contents

Introduction

I'm very well acquainted too with matters mathematical,
I understand equations, both the simple and quadratical.

W. S. Gilbert

Bertrand Russell once said that 'Mathematics may be defined as the subject in which we never know what we are talking about, nor whether what we are saying is true'.

The subject of mathematics can be challenging, fascinating, confusing and frustrating, but once you have developed an interest in the science of numbers, a whole new world is opened up as you discover their many characteristics and patterns.

We all require some numerical skills in our lives, whether it is to calculate our weekly shopping bill or to budget how to use our monthly income, but for many people mathematics is a subject they regard as being too difficult when confronted by what are considered to be its higher branches. When broken down and analysed, and explained in layman's terms, however, many of these aspects can be readily understood by those of us with only a rudimentary grasp of the subject.

The basic purpose of this book is to build up readers' confidence with maths by means of a series of tests and puzzles, which become progressively more difficult over the course of the book, starting with the gentle 'Work out' of Chapter 1 to the collection of 'Complexities and curiosities' of Chapter 8. There is also the opportunity, in Chapter 3, for readers to test their numerical IQ. For many of the puzzles throughout the book, hints towards finding a solution are provided, and in all cases the answers come complete with full detailed explanations.

Many of the problems in this book are challenging, but deliberately so, as the more you practise on this type of puzzle, the more you will come to understand the methodology and thought processes necessary to solve them and the more proficient you will become at arriving at the correct solution. Of equal importance, we set out to show that dealing with numbers can be great fun, and to obtain an understanding of the various aspects of mathematics in an entertaining and informative way can be an uplifting experience.

Section 1
Puzzles, tricks
and tests

Chapter 1

The work out

All intellectual improvement arises from leisure.

Samuel Johnson

Every work out, be it physical or mental, involves a limbering up session.

The puzzles in this chapter are such a limbering up session. They have been specially selected to get you to think numerically and to increase your confidence when working with numbers or faced with a situation in which a mathematical calculation is required, and, like all the puzzles in this book, they are there to amuse and entertain.

When looking at a puzzle, the answer may hit you immediately. If not, your mind must work harder at exploring the options. Mathematics is an exact science, and there is only one correct solution to a correctly set question or puzzle; however, there may be different methods of arriving at that solution, some more laborious than others.

As you work through this first chapter you will find that there are many different ways of tackling this type of puzzle and arriving at a solution, whether it be by logical analysis or by intelligent trial and error.

1 Two golfers were discussing what might have been after they had played a par 5.

Harry said 'if I had taken one shot less and you had taken one shot more, we would have shared the hole'.

Geoff then countered by saying 'yes, and if I had taken one shot less and you had taken one shot more you would have taken twice as many shots as me'.

How many shots did each take?

2 A number between 1 and 50 meets the following criteria:

it is divisible by 3
when the digits are added together the total is between 4 and 8
it is an odd number
when the digits are multiplied together the total is between 4 and 8.

What is the number?

3 On arriving at the party the six guests all say 'Hello' to each other once.

On leaving the party the six guests all shake hands with each other once.

How many handshakes is that in total, and how many 'Hello's?

4 What two numbers multiplied together equal 13?

5 Working at the stable there are a number of lads and lasses looking after the horses. In all there are 22 heads and 72 feet, including all the lads and lasses plus the horses.

If all the lads and lasses and all the horses are sound in body and limb, how many humans and how many horses are in the stable?

6 How many boxes measuring 1 m × 1 m × 50 cm can be packed into a container measuring 6 m × 5 m × 4 m?

7 By what fractional part does four-quarters exceed three-quarters?

8

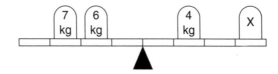

What weight should be placed on x in order to balance the scale?

9 My house number is the lowest number on the street that, when divided by 2, 3, 4, 5 or 6, will always leave a remainder of 1.

However, when divided by 11 there is no remainder.

What is my house number?

10 My brother is less than 70 years old.

The number of his age is equal to five times the sum of its digits. In 9 years time the order of the digits of his age now will be reversed.

How old is my brother now?

11 A greengrocer received a boxful of Brussels sprouts and was furious upon opening the box to find that several had gone bad.

He then counted them up so that he could make a formal complaint and found that 114 were bad, which was 8 per cent of the total contents of the box.

How many sprouts were in the box?

12 If seven men can build a house in 15 days, how long will it take 12 men to build a house assuming all men work at the same rate?

13 At the end of the day one market stall has eight oranges and 24 apples left. Another market stall has 18 oranges and 12 apples left.

What is the difference between the percentages of oranges left in each market stall?

14 Peter is twice as old as Paul was when Peter was as old as Paul is now.

The combined ages of Peter and Paul is 56 years.

How old are Peter and Paul now?

The next two puzzles are of a very similar nature.

15 A bag of potatoes weighs 25 kg divided by a quarter of its weight. How much does the bag of potatoes weigh?

16 One bag of potatoes weighed 60 kg plus one-quarter of its own weight and the other bag weighed 64 kg plus one-fifth of its own weight. Which is the heavier bag?

17

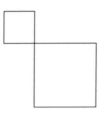

An area of land, consisting of the sums of the two squares, is 1000 square metres.

The side of one square is 10 metres less than two-thirds of the side of the other square.

What are the sides of the two squares?

18 Find four numbers, the sum of which is 45, so that if 2 is added to the first number, 2 is subtracted from the second number, the third number is multiplied by 2 and the fourth number is divided by 2, the four numbers so produced, i.e. the total of the addition, the remainder of the subtraction, the product of the multiplication and the quotient of the division, are all the same.

19 Jack gave Jill as many sweets as Jill had started out with. Jill then gave Jack back as many as Jack had left. Jack then gave Jill back as many as Jill had left. The final exchange meant that poor Jack had none left, and Jill had 80.

How many sweets each did Jack and Jill start out with?

There is a hint to solving this puzzle on page 89.

20 Brian and Ryan are brothers. Three years ago Brian was seven times as old as Ryan. Two years ago he was four times as old. Last year he was three times as old and in two years time he will be twice as old.

How old are Brian and Ryan now?

21 *Sums are not set as a test on Erasmus*

Palindromes have always fascinated *Hannah*. Her boyfriend's name is *Bob*, she lives alone at her cottage in the country named *Lonely Tylenol*, and drives her beloved car, which is *a Toyota*.

A few days ago Hannah was driving along the motorway when she glanced at the mileage indicator and happened to notice that it displayed a palindromic number; 13931.

Hannah continued driving and two hours later again glanced at the odometer, and to her surprise it again displayed another palindrome.

What average speed was Hannah travelling, assuming her average speed was less than 70 mph?

22 The average of three numbers is 17. The average of two of these numbers is 25. What is the third number?

23 You have 62 cubic blocks. What is the minimum number that needs to be taken away in order to construct a solid cube with none left over?

24 I bought two watches, an expensive one and a cheap one. The expensive one cost £200 more than the cheap one and altogether I spent £220 for both. How much did I pay for the cheap watch?

25 If

    6 apples and 4 bananas cost 78 pence

and   7 apples and 9 bananas cost 130 pence

what is the cost of one apple and what is the cost of one banana?

26 The cost of a three-course lunch was £14.00.

The main course cost twice as much as the sweet, and the sweet cost twice as much as the starter.

How much did the main course cost?

27 My watch was correct at midnight, after which it began to lose 12 minutes per hour, until 7 hours ago it stopped completely. It now shows the time as 3.12.

What is now the correct time?

28 A photograph measuring 7.5 cm by 6.5 cm is to be enlarged.

If the enlargement of the longest side is 18 cm, what is the length of the smaller side?

29 A statue is being carved by a sculptor. The original piece of marble weighs 140 lb. On the first week 35% is cut away. On the second week the sculptor chips off 26 lb and on the third week he chips off two-fifths of the remainder, which completes the statue.

What is the weight of the final statue?

30 The ages of five family members total 65 between them.

Alice and Bill total 32 between them
Bill and Clara total 33 between them
Clara and Donald total 28 between them
Donald and Elsie total 7 between them.

How old is each family member?

31 Five years ago I was five times as old as my eldest son. Today I am three times his age.

How old am I now?

32 At my favourite store they are offering a discount of 5% if you buy in cash (which I do), 10% for a long-standing customer (which I am) and 20% at sale time (which it is).

In which order should I claim the three discounts in order to pay the least money?

33 Add you to me, divide by three,
The square of you, you'll surely see,
But me to you is eight to one,
One day you'll work it out my son.

34 In two minutes time it will be twice as many minutes before 1 pm as it was past 12 noon 25 minutes ago.

What time is it now?

35 Find the lowest number that has a remainder of

1 when divided by 2
2 when divided by 3
3 when divided by 4
4 when divided by 5
and   5 when divided by 6.

36
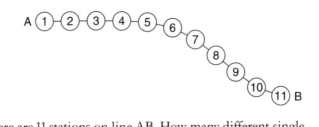

There are 11 stations on line AB. How many different single tickets must be printed to cater for every possible booking from any one of the 11 stations to any other?

37 In a game of eight players lasting for 45 minutes, four reserves alternate equally with each player. This means that all players, including the reserves, are on the pitch for the same length of time.

For how long?

38 Between 75 and 110 guests attended a banquet at the Town Hall and paid a total of £3895.00. Each person paid the same amount, which was an exact number of pounds. How many guests attended the banquet?

39 My sisters April and June each have five children, twins and triplets. April's twins are older than her triplets and June's triplets are older than her twins.

When I saw April recently, she remarked that the sum of the ages of her children was equal to the product of their ages. Later that day I saw June, and she happened to say the same about her children.

How old are my sisters' children?

40 The difference between the ages of two of my three grandchildren is 3.

My eldest grandchild is three times older than the age of my youngest grandchild, and my eldest grandchild's age is also two years more than the ages of my two youngest grandchildren added together.

How old are my three grandchildren?

41 A train travelling at a speed of 50 mph enters a tunnel 2 miles long. The length of the train is $\frac{1}{8}$ mile. How long does it take for all of the train to pass through the tunnel from the moment the front enters to the moment the rear emerges?

There is a hint to this puzzle on page 89.

42 How many minutes is it before 12 noon if 28 minutes ago it was three times as many minutes past 10 am?

43 The highest spire in Great Britain is that of the church of St Mary, called Salisbury Cathedral, in Wiltshire, England. The cathedral was completed and consecrated in 1258; the spire was added from 1334 to 1365 and reaches a height of 202 feet, plus half its own height.

How tall is the spire of Salisbury Cathedral?

44 A manufacturer produces widgets, but not to a very high standard.

In a test batch of 16, five were defective.

Then they carried out a longer production run, in which 25 of 81 were defective.

Had they improved their quality control performance after the test run?

45 A ball is dropped to the ground from a height of 12 feet. It falls to the ground then bounces up half of its original height, then

falls to the ground again. It repeats this, always bouncing back up half of the previous height.

How far has the ball travelled by the time it returns to the ground for the fifth time?

46 In a race of five greyhounds, red jacket, blue, black, striped and white, in how many different ways is it possible for the five dogs to pass the winning post? For example: black, red, white, striped, blue would be one way.

47 A man is playing on the slot machines and starts with a modest amount of money in his pocket. In the first 5 minutes he gets lucky and doubles the amount of money he started with, but in the second 5 minutes he loses £2.00.

In the third 5 minutes he again doubles the amount of money he has left, but then quickly loses another £2.00. He then gets lucky again and doubles the amount of money he has left for the third time, after which he hits another losing streak and loses another £2.00.

He then finds he has no money left.

How much did he start with?

There is a hint to this puzzle on page 89.

48 By permitting just two of the three mathematical signs $(+, -, \times)$ and one other mathematical symbol, plus brackets, can you arrange three fours to equal 100?

There is a hint to this puzzle on page 89.

Chapter 2

Think laterally

If mathematically you end up with the incorrect answer, try multiplying by the page number.

Murphey's Ninth Law

The word *lateral* means of or relating to the side away from the median axis.

Lateral thinking is a method of solving a problem by attempting to look at that problem from many angles rather than search for a direct head-on solution. It involves, therefore, the need to think outside the box and develop a degree of creative, innovative thinking, which seeks to change our natural and traditional perceptions, concepts and ideas. By developing this type of thinking we greatly increase our ability to solve problems that face us, which we could not otherwise solve.

If you cannot solve any of these puzzles at first glance, do not rush to look up the answer, but instead return to the puzzle later to have a fresh look. Sometimes a puzzle that baffles you originally may suddenly appear soluble some hours or even days later.

1 Four explorers in the jungle have to cross a rope bridge at midnight. Unfortunately, the bridge is only strong enough to support two people at a time. Also, because deep in the jungle at midnight it is pitch dark, the explorers require a lantern to guide them, otherwise there is the distinct possibility they would lose their footing and fall to their deaths in the ravine below. However, between them they only have one lantern.

Young Thomas can cross the bridge in 5 minutes, his sister Sarah can cross the bridge in 7 minutes and their father Charles can cross in 11 minutes, but old Colonel Chumpkins can only hobble across in 20 minutes.

How quickly is it possible for all four explorers to reach the other side?

There is a hint to solving this puzzle on page 89.

2 'I will have two boxes of matches at 9 pence each and two bars of soap at 27 pence each', said the customer. 'I will also have three packets of sugar and six Cornish pasties; however, I don't know the price of the sugar or the pasties'.

'Thank you', said the shop assistant, 'that will be £2.92 altogether'.

The customer thought for a few moments, then said, 'that cannot be correct'.

How did she know?

3 Without the use of a calculator, or of pencil and paper, how can you quickly calculate, in your head, the sum of all the numbers from 1 to 1000 inclusive?

4 In my fish tank I have 34 tiger fish. The male fish have 87 stripes each and the female fish have 29 stripes each.

If I take out two-thirds of the male fish, how many stripes in total remain in my fish tank?

5 In a knock-out table-tennis tournament played over one day all players took part who entered, i.e. none of the matches was a walk-over. By the end of the day 39 matches were played before the outright winner emerged.

How many players entered the competition?

There is a hint to solving this puzzle on page 89.

6 A man is walking his dog on the lead towards home at an average of 3 mph. When they are 1.5 miles from home, the man lets the dog off the lead. The dog immediately runs off towards home at an average of 5 mph.

   When the dog reaches the house it turns round and runs back to the man at the same speed. When it reaches the man it turns back for the house.

   This is repeated until the man reaches the house and lets in the dog.

   How many miles does the dog cover from being let off the lead to being let in the house?

7 A company offers a wage increase to its workforce providing the workforce achieves an increase in production of 2.5% per week.

   If the company works a five-day week plus three nights a week overtime and alternate Saturday mornings, by how much per day must the workforce increase production to achieve the desired target?

8 What is the product of

   $$(x - a)(x - b)(x - c)(x - d) \dots (x - z)$$

9 There are 362 880 different possible nine-digit numbers that can be produced using the digits 1 2 3 4 5 6 7 8 9 once each only, and a further 40 320 different possible eight-digit numbers that can be produced using the digits 1 2 3 4 5 6 7 8 once each only $(8 \times 7 \times 6 \times 5 \times 4 \times 3 \times 2 \times 1)$.

How many of these 403 200 different numbers are prime numbers?

There is a hint to solving this puzzle on page 89.

10 I take a certain journey and due to heavy traffic crawl along the first half of the complete distance of my journey at an average speed of 10 mph.

How fast would I have to travel over the second half of the journey to bring my average speed for the whole journey to 20 mph?

11 A snail is climbing out of a well that is 7 foot deep. Every hour the snail climbs 3 feet and slides back 2 feet. How many hours will it take for the snail to climb out of the well?

12 Sue, who has 20 chocolates, and Sally, who has 40 chocolates, decide to share their chocolates equally with Stuart, providing he gives them £1.00.

Stuart agrees and the £1.00 is shared between Sue and Sally according to their contribution.

As a result all the £1.00 went to Sally and none of it to Sue.

Why is this so?

13 How is it possible to arrange three nines to equal 20?

There is a hint to solving this puzzle on page 89.

14

(99) (45) (39) (36) (28) (21)
(72) (27) (18) (21) (?) (13) (7)

Fill in the missing number.

There is a hint to solving this puzzle on page 90.

15 This puzzle involves a census taker and a family with a three-legged pet dog answering to the name of Tripod, who is a key element in finding the solution to the puzzle.

A census taker called on the Smith household in the village and asked Mr Smith for the age of his three daughters.

'Well', said Mr Smith, 'see if you can work this out; if you multiply their ages together you will get a total of 72, and if you add their ages together, you will get a total that is the same as the number on my front door'.

The census taker looked up at the door number and scribbled down some calculations, but after a few minutes said 'I'm afraid that is insufficient information, Mr Smith'.

'I thought you might say that', replied Mr Smith, 'so you should know that my eldest daughter has a pet dog with a wooden leg'.

'Aha! Thank you', said the census taker, 'now I know their ages'.

What were the ages of the three daughters?

There is a hint to solving this puzzle on page 90.

Chapter 3

Test your numerical IQ

An intelligence test (IQ test) is a standardized test designed to measure human intelligence as distinct from attainments. The letters IQ are the abbreviation for intelligence quotient.

Numerical questions are widely used in IQ testing and, as numbers are international, numerical tests are regarded as being culture fair, or culture free, and designed to be free of any particular cultural bias so that no advantage is derived by individuals of one culture relative to those of another.

Such tests, therefore, eliminate language factors or other skills that may be closely tied to another culture, and are frequently designed to test powers of logic, and ability to deal with problems in a structured and analytical way.

Whilst the tests in this chapter have not been standardized we do, nevertheless, provide an approximate guide to performance. Above all, however, the tests are designed to entertain and to increase your confidence when dealing with questions, or a series of questions, of a similar nature.

It is, of course, your choice how you wish to use the tests in this chapter: either to test yourself against the clock, or simply dip into the questions at random and attempt whichever of the questions takes your fancy at the time.

For readers who do wish to assess their performance, a time limit is indicated at the start of each test, which should be adhered to, otherwise your score will be invalidated.

For all, except the numerical matrix test (Test 4) and the mental arithmetic test (Test 5) the use of calculators is permitted.

1 Working with numbers

Time limit 60 minutes

1.1

LEFT

10	7	35	4	11
26	12	18	27	38
15	5	22	40	32
20	8	17	16	29
24	9	3	13	14

RIGHT

26	3	29	35	10
15	12	25	2	7
5	31	17	42	48
28	47	8	19	21
11	20	33	38	4

Multiply the second lowest even number in the left-hand grid by the second highest odd number in the right-hand grid.

1.2

26	7	4	22	16	30
34	45	28	18	10	48
76	38	3	9	36	8
12	4	32	24	14	36
30	52	72	20	1	5
25	2	6	16	64	60

What number is two places away from itself multiplied by 2, four places away from itself less 2, three places away from itself plus 2, and three places away from itself divided by 2?

1.3

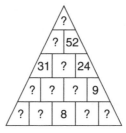

Each number in the pyramid is the sum of the two numbers immediately below it. Fill in the pyramid with the missing numbers.

1.4   In seven years time the combined age of myself and my two sons will be 89. What will it be in 9 years time?

1.5   Divide 250 by a fifth and add 25. How many have you got?

1.6   Sue, Les and John share out a certain sum of money between them. Sue gets $\frac{3}{5}$, Les gets 0.35 and John gets £90.00. How much is the original sum of money?

1.7   47938216478319428697

Add together all the odd numbers in the above list that are immediately followed by an even number.

1.8   Find five consecutive numbers below that total 21.

73426573184393821174526543

1.9

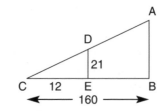

What is the value of line AB?

1.10 Mary has £360 to spend. She spends $\frac{5}{9}$ of the £360.00 in the morning on clothes, 0.375 of the £360.00 in the afternoon on jewellery and writes out a cheque for £95.00 in the evening at a restaurant after taking herself and some friends for a meal.

What is her financial situation at the end of the day?

1.11 What is $\frac{3}{19}$ divided by $\frac{12}{38}$?

1.12 Paul is three times as old as Alice, but in four years time he will only be twice as old.

How old are Paul and Alice now?

1.13 Smith, Jones and Brown supply capital in a new business venture of £15,000, £30,000 and £55,000 respectively and agree to share profits in proportion with the capital invested. Last year £140,000 profits were available. How much profit was allocated to each man?

1.14 Barry is one-and-a-third times the age of Harry. How old are Harry and Barry if their combined ages are 98?

1.15 6297539576821375238862153

What is the average of all the odd numbers greater than 6 in the list above?

2 Series

Fill in the missing number(s) indicated by the question mark in each question.

Time limit 30 minutes

2.1 0, 3, 9, 18, 21, 27, 36, ?

2.2   19, 38, 57, 76, 95, 114, ?

2.3   1, 3, 7, 15, 31, 63, ?

2.4   100, 94.2, 88.4, 82.6, 76.8, ?

2.5   1, 1, 3, 4, 7, 10, 15, ?, 31

2.6   1, 8.5, 9.5, 17, 19, 26.5, 29.5, 37, ?

2.7   6, 18, ?, 60, 62, 186, 188

2.8   100, 98.5, 96, 92.5, 88, ?

2.9   1, 2, 3, 5, 7, 10, 13, ?

2.10 0, 3, −1, 2, −2, 1, −3, ?

2.11 100, 93.25, 86.5, 79.75, ?, 66.25

2.12 10, 10, 12.5, 7.5, ?, 5, 17.5, 2.5

2.13 1, 1, 2, 6, ?, 120, 720

2.14 4, 8, 7, 14, 13, 26, 25, 50, ?, ?

2.15 100, 92, 94, ?, 88, 80, 82, 74

3 Logic

In most of the following questions you must work out which number should replace the question mark in order to meet the same criteria as the remaining sets of numbers in the question.

In questions 3 and 11 you must choose the set of numbers that is the odd set out, that is, they do not meet the same criteria as the remaining numbers in the question.

You have 40 minutes in which to complete the 15 questions.

3.1

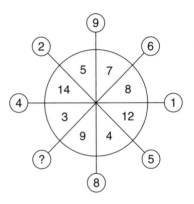

What number should replace the question mark?

3.2

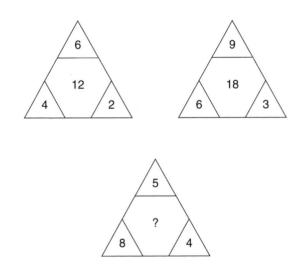

What number should replace the question mark?

3.3

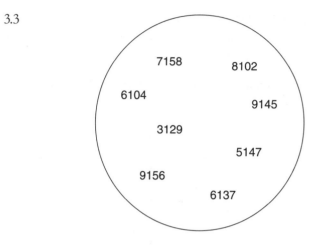

What number is the odd one out?

3.4

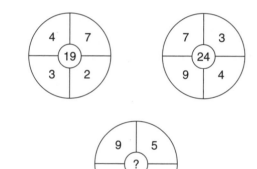

What number should replace the question mark?

3.5

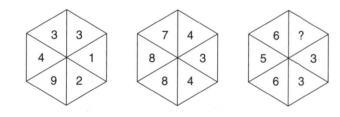

What number should replace the question mark?

3.6

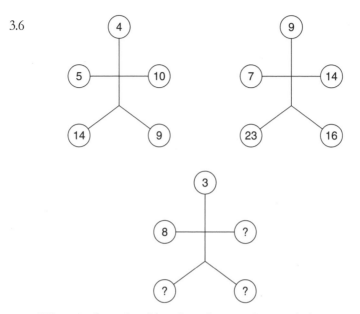

What numbers should replace the question marks?

3.7

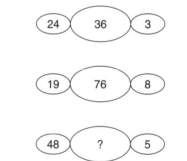

What number should replace the question mark?

3.8

16	7	23	30
12	15	27	42
28	22	50	72
40	37	77	?

What number should replace the question mark?

3.9

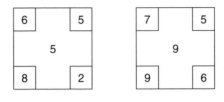

What number should replace the question mark?

3.10

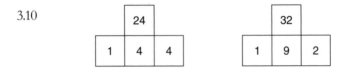

What number should replace the question mark?

3.11

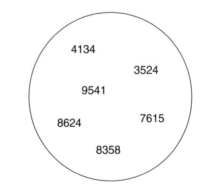

What number is the odd one out?

3.12 54 (117) 36
72 (154) 28
39 (513) 42
18 (?) 71

What number should replace the question mark?

3.13

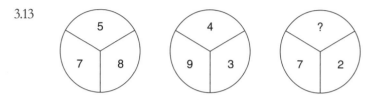

What number should replace the question mark?

3.14

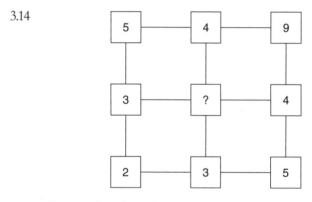

What number should replace the question mark?

3.15

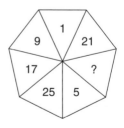

What number should replace the question mark?

4 Numerical matrix test

In all 10 questions in this test a matrix of numbers is displayed with one section missing. From the four choices presented you have to decide, by looking across each line and down each column, or at the matrix as a whole, just what pattern of numbers is occurring, and which should, therefore, be the missing section.

You have 30 minutes in which to complete the 10 questions.

The use of a calculator is not permitted in this test, which is designed to test both your mental agility and powers of logical reasoning.

Example:

1	2	3
4	?	?
7	8	9

Which of the following is the missing section?

6	5		5	2		8	3		5	6

    A   B   C   D

Answer: D.

Explanation:

The numbers 1 2 3 4 5 6 7 8 9 appear reading across each row in turn.

4.1

1	4	7
5	?	11
9	12	?

Which of the following is the missing section?

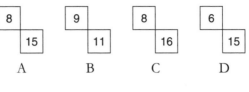

8	9	8	6
15	11	16	15
A	B	C	D

4.2

7	9	2
10	?	5
3	?	3

Which of the following is the missing section?

14	13	15	15
7	6	6	7
A	B	C	D

4.3

7	6	4
?	4	2
4	?	1

Which of the following is the missing section?

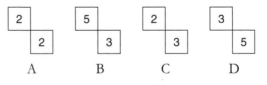

2	5	2	3
2	3	3	5
A	B	C	D

4.4

3	7	6	16
2	4	9	15
5	1	?	?
10	12	22	?

Which of the following is the missing section?

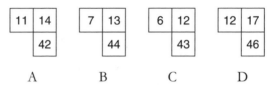

A	B	C	D

4.5

3	8	6	11
1	6	?	9
6	?	9	14
4	9	?	12

Which of the following is the missing section?

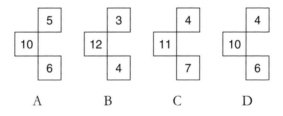

A	B	C	D

4.6

1	2	3	4
3	5	7	?
5	8	?	14
7	11	15	19

Which of the following is the missing section?

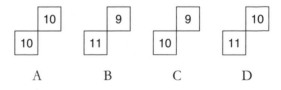

A	B	C	D

4.7

7	8	15	23
4	2	6	8
11	?	?	31
15	?	27	39

Which of the following is the missing section?

10	21
12	

A

12	24
13	

B

10	24
17	

C

14	21
17	

D

4.8

4	7	5	9
3	1	?	3
6	?	7	11
4	2	5	4

Which of the following is the missing section?

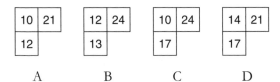

	4
9	

A

	6
8	

B

	5
9	

C

	4
10	

D

4.9

1	5	8	10	11
2	6	9	11	12
4	8	11	?	?
7	11	14	?	17
11	15	?	20	21

Which of the following is the missing section?

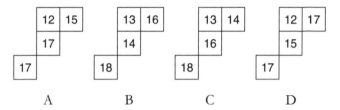

A	B	C	D

4.10

4	7	2	8	14	4
1	3	6	2	6	12
9	5	3	?	10	6
8	14	4	16	?	8
2	6	12	?	12	24
18	10	6	36	?	12

Which of the following is the missing section?

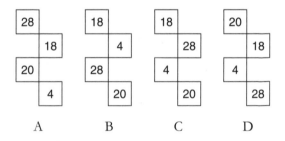

A	B	C	D

5 Mental arithmetic test

It is evident that mental arithmetic is not practised in today's education system to the extent that it was several years ago when children would learn their multiplication tables so well off by heart that they could give the answer to sums such as 7 multiplied by 8 or 6 multiplied by 9 almost without thinking. Perhaps this is not completely surprising due to the widespread use of calculators and computers; nevertheless, we still believe that mental arithmetic is a valuable asset to have at ones disposal and it is also an excellent way of exercising the brain and keeping your mind alert.

The following is a mental arithmetic speed test of 30 questions, which gradually increase in difficulty as the test progresses. Only the answer must be committed to paper, and, of course, the use of calculators is not permitted.

You should work quickly and calmly and try to think at all times of the quickest and most efficient way of tackling the questions.

You have 45 minutes in which to solve the 30 questions.

5.1 What is 7 multiplied by 8?

5.2 What is 102 divided by 3?

5.3 What is 17 multiplied by 11?

5.4 What is 70% of 150?

5.5 Multiply 12 by 8 and divide by 2.

5.6 Divide 72 by 9 and add 15.

5.7 What is 30% of 250?

5.8 What is $\frac{7}{8}$ of 360?

5.9 Multiply 15 by 12 and subtract 23.

5.10 What is $\frac{5}{9}$ of 207 plus 19?

5.11 Multiply 9 by 5 by 8.

5.12 Divide 96 by 4 and add it to 13 multiplied by 3.

5.13 What is 406 divided by 7 then multiplied by 5?

5.14 Add $32 + 19 + 17 + 12 + 15$.

5.15 What is 45% of 720?

5.16 What is $\frac{3}{5}$ of 415?

5.17 Multiply 124 by 21.

5.18 Divide 540 by 12.

5.19 Subtract 927 from 1245.

5.20 Add $\frac{3}{4}$ of 56 to $\frac{3}{5}$ of 85.

5.21 Add $5 + 8 + 15$ and divide by $\frac{1}{8}$ of 112.

5.22 Multiply 70 by 15.

5.23 Add 489 to 357.

5.24 What is 100 divided by 16?

5.25 Multiply 112 by 11.

5.26 Multiply 78 by 9.

5.27 Divide 413 by 59.

5.28 What is $\frac{9}{5}$ expressed as a decimal?

5.29 Add 747 to 978.

5.30 Deduct $\frac{4}{7}$ of 63 from $\frac{5}{9}$ of 117.

Chapter 4

Funumeration

For many people, whose school days were plagued by an intense case of math phobia, mathematics remains what they regard as a dreaded school subject. However, there is no need for this to be the case, especially if the fear factor is replaced by the fun factor, as anything that becomes fun then becomes an enjoyable experience.

Numbers are a universal language that affect all of us in some way in our everyday lives whether we realize it or not, and once you have developed an interest in them, a whole new world is opened up as you discover their many characteristics and patterns.

1 Numbers in wonderland

It is interesting how many numbers have their own individual characteristics.

With some numbers it is possible to tell whether they are a factor of a large number without having to do a division calculation; for example, the tests for divisibility for some even numbers are as follows.

To divide by 2:

a number is always divisible by 2 if the last number is divisible by 2.

To divide by 4:

if the last two digits of any number is divisible by 4, then the number itself is also divisible by 4; for example, 712 688 is divisible by 4 exactly, because 88 is divisible by 4.

To divide by 6:

a number is divisible by 6 exactly if it is divisible by 2 and 3. The test must, therefore, be applied for 2 as explained above and for 3 as explained below. Any even number divisible by 3 is also, therefore, divisible by 6, for example 6, 12, 18, 24 etc.

To divide by 8:

if the last three digits are divisible by 8 exactly, then the number is also divisible by 8.

To divide by 12:

any number is divisible by 12 exactly if it is divisible by 3 and 4 exactly. The test for 3 and 4, therefore, applies.

Tests of divisibility for certain odd numbers are much more intriguing. Examples of such numbers are 3, 9 and 11.

With 3 and 9 all that is necessary is to total up the digits. If their sum is divisible by 3, then that number, or any combination of the same digits, also divides exactly by 3, as in the case of the number 3912, whose digits total 15, which divides by 3 exactly. Similarly, the digits 497 286 total 36, which divides by 9, so the number 497 286, or any combination of these digits, also divides exactly by 9.

A test for 11, which is not so well known, is to see whether the separate sums of alternate digits are equal; for example, the number 746 218 is divisible by 11 exactly, when read either forward or backward, because $7 + 6 + 1 = 4 + 2 + 8$.

There is also a way of finding out whether a number is divisible by 7 or 13. The system is the same for both 7 and 13 and it is to split the number into groups of three starting from the end and insert minus/plus signs alternating from the beginning. For example, $587\ 932 \times 7 = 4\ 115\ 524$ and $4 - 115 + 524 = 413$;

therefore, because 413 is divisible by 7, so is 4 115 524; similarly, 896 712 × 13 = 11 657 256 and 11 − 657 + 256 = −390, so as 390 is divisible by 13, so is 11 657 256.

Another interesting number is 37, because when multiplied it very often produces a palindromic number or, if not palindromic, a number that will divide by 37 when read forward or backward. The reason for this is simply that it is a third of the number 111, and we illustrate its palindromic qualities in puzzle 1.4 below.

Somehow, all the numbers mentioned above, 7, 9, 11, 13, 3 and 37, seem to come together in the magic six digits 142 857. This is the number that fascinated the Reverend Charles Lutwidge Dodgson (1832– 98), who was a lecturer in mathematics at Oxford from 1855 until 1881, but is better known as Lewis Carroll, the author of *Alice's Adventures in Wonderland* (1865).

By dividing 1 by 7 we get the cyclical number 0.142 857 142 857 142 857, and by multiplying together 3 × 9 × 11 × 13 × 37 we get the same recurring digits 142 857. Taking the same six digits Carroll discovered some fascinating characteristics:

142 857 × 1 = 142 857
142 857 × 2 = 285 714
142 857 × 3 = 428 571
142 857 × 4 = 571 428
142 857 × 5 = 714 285
142 857 × 6 = 857 142

The six digits always stay in the same order but move round each time so that each digit occupies each of the six positions. When multiplied by 7 the result is a row of six nines. If you add the first and last three digits the result each time is 999.

It was almost certainly this number that inspired the Mad Hatter's Tea Party in *Alice's Adventures in Wonderland*, which illustrates the idea of cyclic order:

'Let's all move one place on'.

The four puzzles that follow are all based on the above rules of divisibility.

1.1   As demonstrated above, when the sums of the alternate digits of a number are equal, then that number is divisible by 11 exactly.

With this in mind, place the listed digits into the remaining blank spaces in the grid in such a way that each horizontal and vertical line is divisible by 11 exactly when read either forwards or backwards.

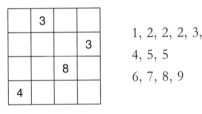

1, 2, 2, 2, 3,
4, 5, 5
6, 7, 8, 9

No multiplication is necessary. All that you must ensure is that the sums of alternate digits in each line and column are equal.

1.2   Although every number that has the sums of alternate digits equal is divisible by 11 exactly, it does not follow that every number that is divisible by 11 exactly has the sums of its digits equal. Are there, therefore, other tests of divisibility?

Take as an example the following numbers:

274 934   6 058 525   2 191 508

All of these numbers are divisible by 11 exactly, even though the sums of their alternate digits are unequal.

There is, however, a further simple rule that will show quickly that these numbers are divisible by 11 exactly without the use of multiplication or division.

By carrying out an analysis of the above three numbers can you determine what this simple rule is?

There is a hint to solving this puzzle on page 90.

1.3   Using the rules already established, can you find, without multiplication or division, both the smallest number and the largest number divisible by 11 exactly to use nine out of the ten digits 0−9 once each only?

There is a hint to solving this puzzle on page 90.

1.4   Now something of a curiosity to illustrate the palindromic qualities of the number 37 that may well have intrigued and amused the Reverend Dodgson considerably.

If the digits 1−9 are placed in the grid as follows:

2	8	4
7	1	9
3	5	6

a total of 16 different numbers will be formed if each horizontal, vertical and corner to corner line is read both forwards and backwards.

Rearrange the digits 1−9 in the grid in such a way that if each of the 16 three-figure numbers are extended to form a palindromic six-figure number (for example 719 917 or 917 719) then each of those 16 six-figure numbers will divide exactly by 37.

There is a hint to solving this puzzle on page 90.

2 Carrolean trickery

Lewis Carroll also figures in our next puzzle, which was in fact a favourite trick of his.

First, write down a four-figure number on a piece of paper, for example 3144 as shown. Now ask a friend to write another four-figure number underneath; for example, your friend may write down the number 2375. You then write down another four-figure number underneath this, that is 7624 as shown, after which your friend writes down a further four-figure number, for example 1738, to which you then add a final four-figure number 8261. Now ask your friend to total up the five numbers to 23 142.

$$
\begin{array}{r}
3144 \\
2375 \\
7624 \\
1738 \\
8261 \\
\hline
23\,142
\end{array}
$$

At this stage you reach in your pocket and pull out a folded piece of paper, ask your friend to open it up, and written on the paper is the number 23 142.

Can you work out how this is done?

3 The two puzzles below are similar in that they have generated much interest and debate over many years. In order to understand how they cause the amount of confusion they do it is not just necessary to consider the validity of the answer, but also to question the validity of the question.

When attempting to solve a puzzle we assume, usually quite correctly, that the question has been correctly stated. However, this is not always the case. A question may be designed in such a way that it attempts to provide a false perception of the problem in order to shift the focus of perspective away from the trap that has been set.

3.1   The famous farmer's horses puzzle

A long time ago a farmer died and left a will stipulating that his 19 horses had to be divided among his three sons. The eldest son, stated the will, was to inherit half, his next son was to have a quarter and his youngest son a fifth, also the will made it clear that none of the horses must be harmed in the division.

While the sons were pondering how it was possible to divide 19 by two, four or five parts without a remainder, a neighbouring farmer rode up, jumped off his horse and put it with the 19, making 20.

He then gave half (10) to the eldest son, a quarter (five) to the second son and a fifth (four) to the youngest son. The 10, five and four horses made 19; the 20th horse was returned to the neighbour, who then departed having done his good deed for the day.

The brothers were all happy as a result but were never able to figure out why to their dying day.

What is the explanation? How was it possible for the neighbour to add his own horse to the others, do the dividing exactly as stated in the will, and have his own horse returned to him at the end?

3.2   The missing £1

Three colleagues went out for a pub lunch and the bill came to £25.00.

Each of the men gave the landlord £10.00 and told him to keep £2.00 out of the change as a tip. The waiter returned with £3.00 and gave each man £1.00.

The meal had, therefore, cost £27.00 plus £2.00 for the tip. Where had the other £1.00 gone?

4 This test is designed to test your powers of mental arithmetic.

1000
  20
  30
1000
1030
1000
  20

Try adding the above numbers up in your head by the following method.

Start by covering the bottom five numbers and adding just the first two numbers. Then uncover one number at a time and add that to the total until you have added up all seven numbers.

Do this just once and do not recheck your answer.

What total have you obtained?

5 With the advent of calculators it became possible to solve complicated equations extremely quickly and to devise ingenious new puzzles.

The two puzzles below are both of a similar nature. If you solve one, you solve them both.

5.1   What animal is represented by this sum?

$$\frac{(12\ 570 + 0.75) \times 16}{333}$$

5.2   A stock market investor sent the coded message below in the form of an equation to his broker to buy shares in a well known company. Having successfully decoded the message the broker bought the shares. In which company?

$$\left((2843 \times 5) + \frac{7.035}{15} \right) \times 5$$

6   The following trick gives your age in the year 2003, when this book was written. What adjustment needs to be made for it to work in the year 2004, the year of publication, and in subsequent years?

First of all choose a number (for ease of calculation you may wish to choose between 2 and 9)

Multiply by 2

Add 5

Multiply by 50

If you have had a birthday this year add 1753, otherwise add 1752

Now subtract the four-digit year that you were born

You should now have a three-digit number

The first digit of this is your original number and the last two digits are your current age.

7   The following number trick demonstrates further properties of the number 9.

Ask a friend to think of a four-digit number where all the digits are different.

Now ask them to add up all of the four digits and subtract the sum of the digits from the original number.

Now add up the digits of the result.

Ask them whether the answer is one-digit or a two-digit number. If it is one digit tell them the answer is 9 (it always will be). If the answer is two digits then ask them to add the two digits together. Then tell them the answer obtained is 9 (it always will be).

8 Trick numbers

We will explore magic number squares in more detail later in this chapter.

There are, however, other forms of magic square, of which the array of numbers below is an example.

19	16	11	13	9
17	14	9	11	7
20	17	12	14	10
15	12	7	9	5
22	19	14	16	12

19	(16)	11	13	9
17	14	9	11	7
20	17	12	14	10
15	12	7	9	5
22	19	14	16	12

To show how this array of numbers reveals magic properties, give someone a folded piece of paper with the number 66 written on it. Ask them not to look at the number at that stage. Now ask them to pick any number in the square and put a circle round the number they have chosen. Then cross out every other number across the same row and down the same column; for example, if the number 16 had been chosen you would circle the number 16, and cross out numbers 19, 11, 13 and 9 (across the same row) and 14, 17, 12 and 19 (down the same column).

Now ask them to pick a second number from the ones not already crossed out and repeat the same process. Then repeat the process a third and a fourth time, after which only one number will remain not crossed out, and this number is then also circled. Now total up the five circled numbers, which have apparently been selected at random, and ask your *victim* to look at the number written on the folded piece of paper to reveal the same answer – 66.

No matter how many times the process is repeated with the same array of numbers, the answer will always be the same – 66!

Why is this so?

9 Think of a number

Now double it

Add 4

Multiply by 5

Add 12

Multiply by 10

From the answer, how can you always work out quickly the original number?

10 Think of a number

Multiply it by 4

Add 2

Multiply by 5

From the result how is it possible to determine the original number very quickly?

11 This number trick enables you to tell someone the date, month and year of birth.

Take the number corresponding to the month of the year in which you were born (for example: August = 8)

Multiply by 100

Add the date of the month on which you were born

Multiply by 2

Add 8

Multiply by 5

Add 4

Multiply by 10

Add 4

Add your age

From the result deduct 444. Now group the digits in pairs from the right. The first pair is your age, the second pair is the date of the month and the last pair (or one) is the month.

For example: 10/06/45 (age 45, birthday 6 October)

12 Magic number squares

Magic number squares have intrigued mathematicians and puzzle fanatics for centuries. Perfect magic number squares must use consecutive numbers, each one only once, to produce the same total across each horizontal line, down each vertical line and from corner to corner, as in the simplest array of numbers below, which uses the numbers 1–9 once each only to produce the total 15 in each horizontal, vertical and corner-to-corner line.

8	1	6
3	5	7
4	9	2

The above example dates from around the beginning of the 10th century AD and is part of the Chinese Loh River scroll. The lo-shu is unique because there is only one possible solution, not counting reflections and rotations, of which there are seven additional versions.

As the order of magic squares increases, so do the number of different possible versions, for example not counting rotations and reflections there are 800 different order four squares and over 275 million order five squares, of which just one example is shown below.

17	5	10	20	13
16	23	14	8	4
11	7	1	25	21
2	24	18	9	12
19	6	22	3	15

There is a formula for working out the sum of the rows of each magic square. To obtain the constant of a standard order four square, add the integers from 1 to 16 and divide the sum by 4 – the constant is 34. The constant of an order five square is the sum of the numbers 1–25 divided by 5 – i.e. 65.

A further simple formula is that the constant $= \frac{1}{2} \times$ (order cubed + order). Thus for an order six square, as illustrated below, the constant is $(6 \times 6 \times 6) + 6$ divided by $2 = 111$.

24	19	26	6	1	35
25	23	21	7	32	3
20	27	22	2	9	31
15	10	17	33	28	8
16	14	12	34	5	30
11	18	13	29	36	4

However, there is also another check that will determine the constant for any size of magic square, which can also be used as a number trick similar to puzzle 8 (trick numbers).

The way this works is as follows.

First create a 3 × 3 number grid and write the numbers:

1	2	3
4	5	6
7	8	9

Now circle any number and cross out all the other numbers in the same row and column.

Repeat the process using numbers not already circled or crossed out. Now there should be just one number left, which should also be circled. For example:

Now add up the three circled numbers. The answer will always be 15, which is the constant for a 3 × 3 magic square.

The system works for any size of grid created in this way, as in the order 10 magic square below, which has a constant of 505.

1	2	3	4	5	6	7	8	9	10
11	12	13	14	15	16	17	18	19	20
21	22	23	24	25	26	27	28	29	30
31	32	33	34	35	36	37	38	39	40
41	42	43	44	45	46	47	48	49	50
51	52	53	54	55	56	57	58	59	60
61	62	63	64	65	66	67	68	69	70
71	72	73	74	75	76	77	78	79	80
81	82	83	84	85	86	87	88	89	90
91	92	93	94	95	96	97	98	99	100

92	99	1	8	15	67	74	51	58	40
98	80	7	14	16	73	55	57	64	41
4	81	88	20	22	54	56	63	70	47
85	87	19	21	3	60	62	69	71	28
86	93	25	2	9	61	68	75	52	34
17	24	76	83	90	42	49	26	33	65
23	5	82	89	91	48	30	32	39	66
79	6	13	95	97	29	31	38	45	72
10	12	94	96	78	35	37	44	46	53
11	18	100	77	84	36	43	50	27	59

The following is a selection of four magic square puzzles.

12.1

1	2	3	4
5	6	7	8
9	10	11	12
13	14	15	16

Change the position of just four pairs of numbers to convert the above into a magic square where each horizontal, vertical and corner-to-corner line totals 34.

12.2

96	11	89	68
88	69	91	16
61	86	18	99
19	98	66	81

The above square has a constant of 264. Can you find two other unusual features that it possesses?

12.3   This puzzle contains three magic squares in one. Several numbers have been inserted already and your task is to insert the remaining numbers from 1 to 49 so that each row, column and corner-to-corner line adds up to 175. In addition, the middle 3 × 3 square should add up to 75, and the inner 5 × 5 square should add up to 125.

	9		47		49	10
38		20			35	
39						11
	36		25			
6		28				44
			33		31	
	41		3			

12.4   The grid below contains the numbers 1–16 once each only; however, only five of the lines add up to 34. Your task is to divide the square into four sections of equal size and shape and then to re-assemble the four sections to form a true magic square, in which each horizontal, vertical and corner-to-corner line totals 34.

13	7	10	4
15	2	12	5
8	9	3	14
1	11	6	16

Chapter 5

Think logically

A definition of logical is analytic or deductive, and this definition can be applied to someone who is capable of using reason in an orderly cogent fashion.

All the puzzles in this section can be solved by logical analysis. There is no specialized knowledge required in order to solve these puzzles, just a requirement to think logically and follow an argument step by step in a structured and analytical way through to its conclusion.

1

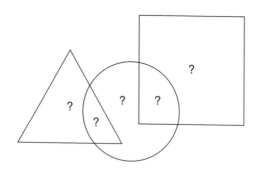

The question marks represent five consecutive numbers.

When added together:

The numbers in the triangle = 35

The numbers in the square = 29

What numbers replace the question marks?

2 The family next door has both girl and boy children. Each of the boys has the same number of brothers as he has sisters and each of the girls has twice as many brothers as she has sisters.

How many boys and girls are there?

3 In many puzzles certain assumptions have to be made. In this puzzle the assumption is that trains arrive at their destination precisely on time. The puzzle, therefore, can only work in theory.

My wife usually leaves work at 16.30 hours, calls at the supermarket, then catches the 17.00 train, which arrives at our local station at 17.30. I leave home each day, drive to the station and pick up my wife at 17.30, just as she gets off the train. One day last week my wife was able to finish work about five minutes earlier than usual, decided to go straight to the station instead of calling at the supermarket, and managed to catch the 16.30 train, which arrived at our local station at 17.00. Because I was not there to pick her up she began to walk home. I left home at the usual time, saw my wife walking, turned round, picked her up, and drove home, arriving there 12 minutes earlier than usual.

For how long did my wife walk before I picked her up?

4 A man jogs at 6 mph over a certain journey and walks back over the same route at 4 mph.

What is his average speed for the journey?

There is a hint to solving this puzzle on page 90.

5 I set both my wife's watch and my watch at midnight. It later transpired that one of the watches went, on average, two minutes per hour too slow, and the other went, on average, one minute per hour too fast, as when I looked at them later the same day, the faster one was exactly one hour ahead of the other.

What was the correct time when I looked at the watches?

6

Place the numbers 1–6 inclusive in the circles so that

the sum of the numbers 5 and 6 and all the numbers between them is 15

the sum of the numbers 1 and 2 and all the numbers between them is 12

the sum of the numbers 5 and 4 and all the numbers between them is 21.

There is a hint to solving this puzzle on page 90.

7 A new European Community directive fining motorists for speeding had a somewhat incomprehensible formula by which each motorist's fine was assessed.

Basically, the formula involved using the ten digits 0–9 once each only and making two five-digit totals. Then, by subtracting one from the other, the difference would be the amount of each fine in Euros.

What is the smallest amount a motorist could be fined by using this method?

There is a hint to solving this puzzle on page 90.

8 A batsman is out for 23 runs, which raises his batting average for the season from 15 to 16. How many runs would he have had to have scored to bring his average up to 18?

9 The chambermaid had mixed up the keys to the 20 rooms.

What is the *maximum* number of times she needs to try a key in a door in order to sort out which key opens which door?

There is a hint to solving this puzzle on page 91.

10   A man has 45 socks in his drawer, 14 identical blue, 24 identical red and 7 identical black.

The lights are fused and he is completely in the dark.

How many socks must he take out to make certain he has a pair of each colour?

11   Your boss offers you a choice of two options by which your new salary is to be calculated.

First option:

initial salary £30,000 to be increased after each 12 months by £1000.00

Second option:

initial salary £30,000 to be increased after each 6 months by £250.00

Your salary is to be calculated every 6 months.

Which option should you choose?

12   At the end of the year five ladies of the Enigma Weight-Watchers Club went on the scales two at a time and every possible combination of two ladies was recorded, which resulted in 10 separate weighings.

The 10 weighings were as follows:

110 kg, 112 kg, 113 kg, 114 kg, 115 kg, 116 kg, 117 kg, 118 kg, 120 kg and 121 kg.

How much did each lady weigh?

There is a hint to solving this puzzle on page 91.

13

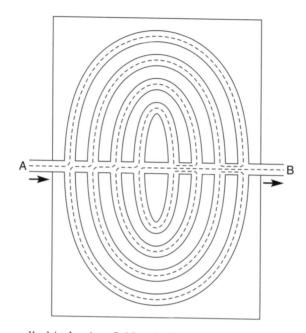

A man walks his dog in a field each day from the point A where he enters the field to the point B where he exits. The field has four circular paths and each day he walks round every one of the circular paths in order to give himself and his dog plenty of exercise.

How many possible different routes are there by which he is able to do this? One such route is shown by the dotted line, but how many more are there?

His walk must take him over every one of the four paths and although inevitably he does arrive at the same intersection more than once on his travels, he does not go over any part of the paths twice.

There is a hint to solving this puzzle on page 91.

14 I have a set of eight weights, which, by using a set of scales where the weights are placed in one pan and the object to be weighed placed in the other pan, enables me to weigh objects to the accuracy of 1 g, starting with 1 g, up to an object weighing 255 g. What is the value of each of the weights?

There is a hint to solving this puzzle on page 91.

15 There are 100 nuts in five trays (five different kinds of nut).

Tray 1 plus tray 2 = 52 nuts
Tray 2 plus tray 3 = 43 nuts
Tray 3 plus tray 4 = 34 nuts
Tray 4 plus tray 5 = 30 nuts

How many nuts does each tray contain?

There is a hint to solving this puzzle on page 91.

Chapter 6

The logic of gambling and probability

Man has always been a gambler. The urge to beat the odds is inherent in most people, and in the 17th century the French philosopher, mathematician and physicist Blaise Pascal formulated the first rules relating to probability.

It was in 1654 that Antoine Chevalier de Mere asked Pascal why he usually lost when he bet even money that a double 6 would show up at least once in 24 rolls of two dice. Pascal demonstrated that 24 rolls would be against the gambler, but 25 rolls would be slightly in his favour.

Up to then gambling odds were arrived at by trial and error. Pascal, however, was able to calculate the odds of chance in a scientific way.

The basic rules are really quite simple. Calculate the chances that an event will happen and then calculate the chances that it will not happen. For example: what are the odds against drawing a named card out of a pack of 52?

The probability of drawing the named card is $\frac{1}{52}$. The probability of not drawing the named card is $\frac{51}{52}$. The odds in favour of drawing the named card is in the ratio of the first probability to the second, that is, $\frac{1}{52}$ to $\frac{51}{52}$, or 1 to 51.

In America, during the gold-rush era, there was a very ingenious gambling game that was a favourite of the Wild West card sharps, and thousands of dollars were won from the unsuspecting gold prospectors. In a saloon the gambler would gather a crowd and into a hat would be placed three cards. These cards were coloured as follows.

Card 1:   Gold on one side   Gold on reverse
Card 2:   Silver on one side   Silver on reverse
Card 3:   Gold on one side   Silver on reverse

The gambler then asked the onlooker to draw a card from the hat and place it on the table.

If, for example, the card was placed *gold* side up, the gambler would say 'The reverse side is either gold or silver as the card cannot be the silver/silver card. It is, therefore, either the gold/silver card or the gold/gold card, an even chance! I will bet even money one dollar that the reverse side is gold'.

The snag here, and the reason why the odds were heavily in favour of the gambler and stacked against the punter by 2–1, in other words he will lose two games out of three, is that we are not dealing with cards but with sides.

There were six sides to begin with, three of each:

Gold	Silver
1	
1	
	1
	1
1	1
$\frac{}{3}$	$\frac{}{3}$

The card on the table cannot be the silver/silver card, so by eliminating that one we are left with

Gold	Silver
1	
1	
1	1
$\frac{}{3}$	$\frac{}{1}$

The following puzzles are all based on the laws of probability.

1 A car manufacturer produces only red and blue models, which
come out of the final testing area completely at random. What are
the odds that five consecutive cars of the same colour will come
through the test area at any one time?

2 A hand in bridge in which all 13 cards are a nine or below is
called a Yarborough, after the second Earl of Yarborough
(d. 1897), who is said to have bet 1000 to 1 against the dealing of
such a hand. What, however, are the actual odds against such a
hand? Was the noble lord onto a good thing?

3 If two standard six-sided dice are thrown, their total score could
be anything from 2 to 12. Which would be likely to appear more
often over a long period, 9 or 10?

4 Four balls are placed in a bag. One is white, one is black and the
other two are red. The bag is shaken and someone draws two
balls from the bag. He looks at the two balls and announces that
one of them is red. What are the chances that the other ball he has
drawn out is also red?

There is a hint to solving this puzzle on page 91.

5 If you toss a coin in the air it is a $\frac{50}{50}$, or even money, chance that it
will land heads upwards and an even money chance that it will
land tails upwards.

Now suppose you toss five coins in the air together and are
betting on the outcome.

What are the chances that at least four of the coins will land
either all heads or all tails upwards?

6 The French mathematician d'Alembert (1717–83) considered the possibility of throwing heads at least once when tossing a coin twice. 'There are only three possible cases', he argued.

Case 1: tails appears on the first toss and again on the second toss
Case 2: tails appears on the first toss and heads on the second toss
Case 3: heads appears on the first toss (therefore in case 3 there is no longer need to carry out the second toss).

'It is, therefore, quite simple,' he stated, 'as there are only three possible cases, in which two of these are favourable, the probability is 2 out of 3'.

Obviously his reasoning was correct, or was it?

There is a hint to solving this puzzle on page 91.

7 You have two bags each containing eight balls. The first bag contains balls numbered 1–8 and the second bag contains balls numbered 9–16.

A ball is drawn out of bag one and another ball out of bag two.

What are the chances that at least one of the balls drawn out is an odd numbered ball?

8 A man went to a drawer in complete darkness for a pair of white socks. In the drawer he had only white socks and black socks, and he had just four socks in the drawer.

He took out a pair of socks. The chances that they were a pair of white socks was one in two or $\frac{50}{50}$, an even money chance.

What were the chances that the pair of socks was black?

Chapter 7

Geometrical puzzles

A straight line is the shortest distance between two points.

The sum of the interior angles of any triangle is equal to the sum of two right angles.

The square of the hypotenuse of a right-angled triangle is equal to the sum of the squares of the other two sides.

(Pythagorean theorem)

God geometrizes continually.

(Plato)

Whilst the solution to many puzzles in this book will provide a great deal of intellectual pleasure to the reader, there is nothing in mathematics which is so aesthetically pleasing as geometric dissection puzzles, to which the second half of this chapter is devoted.

1

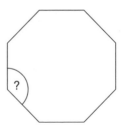

What is the value of the internal angle of an octagon?

There is a hint to solving this puzzle on page 91.

2 Lines AB and BC are two diagonals drawn on the face of a cube.

How many degrees is the angle created by ABC?

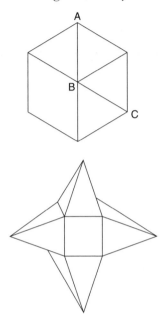

3

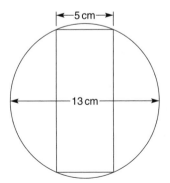

A ufologist recently reported a strange object, which he described as being in the shape of a quasi-pyramid, hovering over a cornfield.

If you add the number of edges this figure has to its number of faces, what total do you arrive at?

4

A solid steel round ball, 13 cm in diameter has a 5 cm hole drilled through the centre.

How deep is the hole?

There is a hint to solving this puzzle on page 91.

5

At each stage the arrow moves three places clockwise and the star moves four places anti-clockwise.

After how many stages will the arrow and the star appear together in the same segment?

6 Geometrical dissections

Mathematicians pondered for centuries whether basic two-dimensional shapes (polygons) could be cut and reassembled to make different shapes.

The basic shapes that they considered, in order of complexity, are

1 sided	circle	6 sided	hexagon
2 sided	semi-circle	7 sided	heptagon
3 sided	triangle	8 sided	octagon
4 sided	square	9 sided	nonagon
5 sided	pentagon	10 sided	decagon

By the middle of the 20th century the results had been summarized as shown in the chart below:

FROM:

	TRIANGLE	SQUARE	PENTAGON	HEXAGON	HEPTAGON	OCTAGON	NONAGON	DECAGON	DODECAGON	GREEK CROSS	LATIN CROSS	MALTESE CROSS	PENTAGRAM
SQUARE	4												
PENTAGON	6	6											
HEXAGON	5	5	7										
HEPTAGON	9	9	11	11									
OCTAGON	8	5	9	9	13								
NONAGON	9	12		14									
DECAGON	8	8	10	9	13	12							
DODECAGON	8	6		6									
GREEK GROSS	5	4	7	7	12	9		10	6				
LATIN CROSS	5	5	8	6	12	8		10	7	7			
MALTESE CROSS		7		14							9		
PENTAGRAM	9	8		10				6					
HEXAGRAM	5	5	8	7	11	9		9	10	8	9		

TO:

For example, a hexagon can be dissected into five pieces and reassembled to form a square as follows, and vice versa:

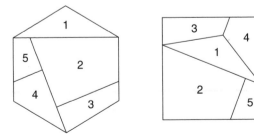

An octagon can be dissected into five pieces that can be reassembled to form a square as follows, and vice versa:

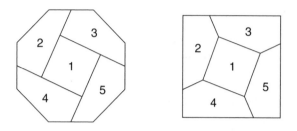

And a hexagram can be dissected into five pieces that can be reassembled to form a triangle, and vice versa:

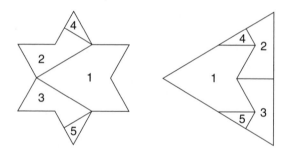

Now try the following related puzzles.

6.1 Dissect a triangle and reassemble the pieces to form a square.

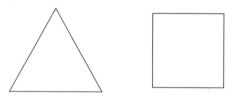

6.2 Take a quarter away from a square and dissect the remaining three quarters into four congruent (same size and shape) pieces.

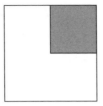

6.3 Take a quarter away from a triangle and dissect the remaining three quarters into four congruent (same size and shape) pieces.

7

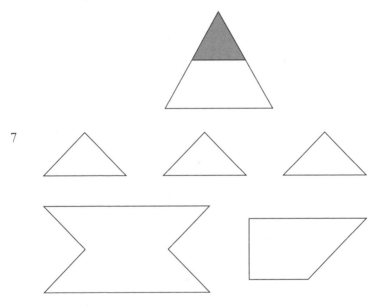

Arrange the five pieces into the shape of a cross.

There is a hint to solving this puzzle on page 92.

8

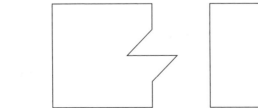

Cut the shape on the left into four pieces of identical shapes to form the square.

There is a hint to solving this puzzle on page 92.

9

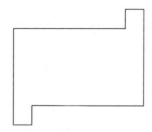

Cut the shape into two pieces that when fitted together will form a rectangle.

There is a hint to solving this puzzle on page 92.

Chapter 8

Complexities and curiosities

Whilst several of the puzzles in this section do involve a degree of complexity, they do not involve any specialized knowledge; in other words, each one of us is capable of solving the puzzle without the need to be aware of some specific formula.

Whilst both puzzles and problems frequently involve the same sort of thought process in order to reach a solution, there is a subtle difference between puzzles and problems.

A puzzle is set by another person, and has a solution that is already known to that person. It is a puzzle, for example, to ask a question such as *what number is 35 less than six times itself*, and a correctly set puzzle should have just one solution which has been worked out by the puzzle setter, even though there often may be several different ways of arriving at that solution.

A problem, on the other hand, arises in life. It is not set artificially and there is not an answer already known to someone else. There is no right answer but some solutions may be better than others.

Whilst some may prefer one to the other, both puzzles and problems can bring their rewards. Undoubtedly the successful resolution of a problem achieves a worthwhile goal and, apart from their recreational value, we believe the major reward to be obtained from tackling puzzles is that they stretch and exercise the mind, and enable you to tackle the real problems of life with vigour and confidence.

The first part of this chapter contains a selection of brainteasers, which involve different kinds of thought process. For the more difficult puzzles hints are provided and detailed explanations, where necessary, are provided with the answers.

In the second part we present a number of curiosities in the form of puzzles to demonstrate the unusual and sometimes unique qualities possessed by many numbers.

The complexities

1 Which four-figure number, consisting of four different digits, meets the following criteria?

The first digit is twice the value of the fourth digit and two more than the second digit. The third digit is one more than the first digit and five more than the fourth digit.

2 Sally visits four stores in a day long shopping spree with a handbag full of money.

In the first store she spends £10.00 in the first half hour, half the money she had left in the second half hour and £10.00 in the third half hour. She repeats this throughout all four stores and leaves the fourth store having spent all the money she started out with.

How much money did she start out with?

There is a hint to solving this puzzle on page 92.

3 Sid and Jim were engaged by the local council to paint yellow lines on either side of a certain street. Sid arrived first and had painted three metres on the right-hand side when Jim arrived and pointed out that Sid should be painting the left-hand side. So Sid started afresh on the left-hand side and Jim continued what Sid had started on the right.

When Jim had finished his side he went across the street and painted six metres for Sid, which finished the job. Both sides of the street were an equal length.

Who painted the greatest distance, and by how much?

There is a hint to solving this puzzle on page 92.

4 1, 81, 2025, ?, 9801, 88 209, 494 209, 998 001, 4 941 729

What do the above numbers all have in common, and which number is missing?

There is a hint to solving this puzzle on page 92.

5 In a recent election for mayor, a total of 46 298 votes were cast for the five candidates, the winner beating his opponents by 2648, 5216, 7141 and 10 692 votes respectively.

How many votes were cast for each candidate?

6 The delectable number

Numbers can be divided into many different categories: a few of these we would like to expound on are amicable, abundant, deficient, perfect and delectable.

Amicable numbers are pairs that are mutually equal to the sum of all their aliquot parts, for example 220 and 284. The aliquot parts of 220 are 1, 2, 4, 5, 10, 11, 20, 22, 44, 55 and 110, the sum of which is 284, while the aliquot parts of 284 are 1, 2, 4, 71 and 142, the sum of which is 220. There are seven known pairs of amicable numbers:

220	284
1184	1210
5020	5564
6232	6368
10 744	10 856
17 926	18 416
9 437 056	9 363 584

Abundant, deficient and perfect numbers can be linked together as every number is one of these. An abundant number is one such that the sum of all its divisors (except itself) is greater than the number itself: for example 12, because its divisors 1, 2, 3, 4 and 6 total 16. Opposite to this is a deficient number, where the divisors total less than the number itself: for example 10, where its divisors, 1, 2 and 5, total 8.

If a number is not abundant or deficient, then it must be perfect, which means that it is equal to the sum of its aliquot parts: for example 6, where its divisors 1, 2 and 3, also total 6. Perfect numbers were first named in ancient Greece by the Pythagoreans around 500 BC, and to date only 30 have been discovered. The first four were discovered before AD 100 and they are 6, 28, 496 and 8028. However, the next was not found until the 15th century, and is 33 550 336, and the latest to be discovered, by means of computer technology, has no fewer than 240 digits.

So, having dealt with amicable, abundant, deficient and perfect numbers, what then is a delectable number? The answer is that a nine-digit number is delectable if

(i)   it contains the digits 1–9 exactly once each (no zero) and
(ii) the numbers created by taking the first n digits (n runs from 1 to 9) are each divisible by n.

So, the first digit is divisible by 1 (it always will be), the first two digits form a number divisible exactly by 2, the first three digits form a number divisible exactly by 3 and so on.

It is known that there is one, and only one, nine-digit number that meets the above conditions and thus earns itself the title the delectable number. Can you find it?

7 Between my patio and my lawn is a narrow strip of grass separating two flower-beds.

Recently, I watched a convoy of 10 snails cross this piece of grass and measured the length of time that the whole process took, which was precisely 50 minutes. This was the time from the instant the first snail slithered onto the grass to the instant the last snail left the grass. The snails crossed in single file and the piece of grass is only long enough to accommodate eight snails at any one time.

The snails travelled at the same speed and each snail was on the lawn for the same length of time.

For how long was each snail on the lawn, from the instant its front made contact with the lawn to the instant its tail left the lawn?

There is a hint to solving this puzzle on page 92.

8   The following are two related puzzles.

   8.1   A gardener had fewer than 500 plant pots of chrysanthemum cuttings, which he was trying to arrange as neatly as possible on his greenhouse staging.

   First he tried arranging them in rows of two, but found there was one left over. Then he tried them in rows of three, but again there was 1 left over. Likewise he tried them in rows of four, then five, then six and always found one left over.

   Finally he tried them in rows of seven and this time the rows were exactly even.

   How many plant pots did he have?

   8.2   There were between 2200 and 2600 guests invited to the Lord Mayor's civic luncheon. The organizer decided he would arrange the seating so that each table would seat an equal number of guests, and the number of guests at each table would be an odd number.

The organizer worked out that three guests per table would not work as two guests would be left over, neither would five per table, which would leave four guests without a table, neither would seven per table, which would leave six over, and nine per table would leave eight over.

However, when he tried seating 11 guests per table it worked exactly, and none were left over.

How many guests in total were invited to the luncheon?

9

Insert numbers into the remaining blank squares so that the sums in each line and column are correct.

10 These fractions all have a certain feature in common. Can you say what it is?

$$\frac{16}{64} \qquad \frac{19}{95} \qquad \frac{26}{65}$$

11 The number of the beast

Rev 13 : 18 Here is wisdom. Let him that hath understanding count the number of the beast; for it is the number of a man, and his number Six hundred threescore six.

The number of 666 is made famous by the *Book of Revelation* (Chapter 13, verse 18), and it has also been studied extensively by mathematicians because of the many interesting properties it reveals, a few examples being listed below.

The number 666 is the sum and difference of the first three sixth powers:

$$666 = 1^6 - 2^6 + 3^6 \qquad (1 - 64 + 729 = 666)$$

It is also equal to the sum of its digits plus the cubes of its digits:

$$666 = 6 + 6 + 6 + 6^3 + 6^3 + 6^3 \qquad (6^3 = 216)$$

666 is the sum of two successive prime numbers: $313 + 353$

The sum of the squares of the first seven primes is 666:

$$666 = 2^2 + 3^2 + 5^2 + 7^2 + 11^2 + 13^2 + 17^2$$

If you write the first six Roman numerals in order from largest to smallest, you get

$$DCLXVI = 666$$

If you write down the phrase 'expect the devil' and then extract the Roman numerals from that phrase, i.e. X (10), C (100), D (500), V (5), I (1), L (50), their total is 666.

11.1 There are two ways to insert + signs into the sequence 123456789 in order to produce the number 666, and just one way for the sequence 987654321.

Can you find them?

11.2 In the alphametic below, replace the letters with digits (i.e. S must be replaced by the same number throughout the sum etc) so that the addition sum is correct.

$$\begin{array}{r} \text{SIX} \\ \text{SIX} \\ \text{SIX} \\ + \text{BEAST} \\ \hline \text{SATAN} \end{array}$$

There is a hint to solving this puzzle on page 92.

12 A cardboard box manufacturer was considering doubling the volume of his square boxes. On learning of this his supplier of cardboard, hearing that he was seeking quotes from other suppliers, decided to encourage him to place the extra business with him by offering a generous 37.5% quantity discount on his new total turnover figure.

How much extra would the box manufacturer have to pay for the additional cardboard if he placed the business with his regular supplier and enjoyed the new 37.5% quantity discount?

There is a hint to solving this puzzle on page 92.

13 The number 27 can be represented by a mixed fraction using the digits 1–9 once each only in the following way:

$$15\ \frac{9432}{786}$$

Thus 9432 divided by 786 equals 12, and $12 + 15 = 27$

Can you find a similar arrangement to represent the number 16, and then a further arrangement to represent the number 20? In each solution the digits 1–9 may only be used once each only.

There is a hint to solving this puzzle on page 93.

14 In this addition sum, only one out of the five decimal points is in the correct position. Alter the four incorrect decimal points to make the sum add up correctly.

47.5
38.627
125.4
1583.3
———
4508.57

15

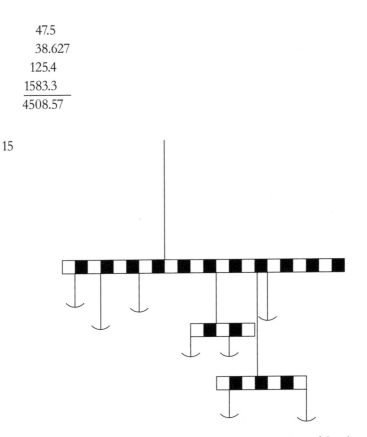

Put eight weights of 1 g, 2 g, 3 g, 4 g, 5 g, 6 g, 7 g and 8 g into the eight pans to make the scale balance.

16 Out of 100 ladies surveyed

85 had a white handbag
75 had black shoes
60 carried an umbrella
90 wore a ring

How many ladies at least must have had all four items?

There is a hint to solving this puzzle on page 93.

17 Insert the numbers 1–7 in the circles, so that for any particular
circle the sum of the numbers in the circles connected directly to
it equals the value corresponding to the number in that circle, as
given in the list.

Example:

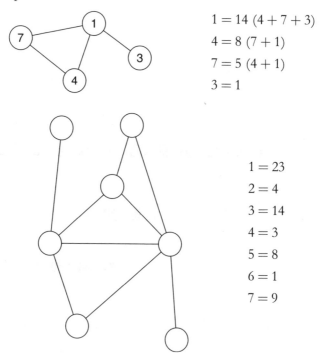

$1 = 14 \ (4 + 7 + 3)$

$4 = 8 \ (7 + 1)$

$7 = 5 \ (4 + 1)$

$3 = 1$

$1 = 23$

$2 = 4$

$3 = 14$

$4 = 3$

$5 = 8$

$6 = 1$

$7 = 9$

There is a hint to solving this puzzle on page 93.

18 This puzzle is sometimes referred to as the birthday paradox and
explains why, in many large families it is no great coincidence
when family members share the same birthday, for example, one
of the authors of this book shares a birthday with his cousin's son
(3 January) albeit about 30 years apart.

Twenty-four people attend the Golf Club AGM. The probability
that two of these people, chosen completely at random, share the

same birthday is 1 in 365, or 364 to 1 because, disregarding leap years, there are 365 days in a year.

However, it may surprise you to learn that the chances of any two of the 24 people sharing the same birthday is approximately an even money chance.

How can this be so?

19 The two puzzles that follow both involve a similar thought process.

19.1 A number of aliens, who have just dropped in from another planet, emerge from their spacecraft.

(i)   There is more than one alien
(ii)   each alien has the same number of fingers
(iii)   each alien has at least one finger on each hand
(iv)   the total number of fingers of all the aliens is between 200 and 300
(v)   if you knew the total number of fingers of all the aliens, you would know how many aliens there are.

How many aliens are there?

There is a hint to solving this puzzle on page 93.

19.2 In the wood are a number of trees. Once upon a time each tree had a number of birds in its branches and there were at least two birds to each tree, and, in the most amazing of all coincidences, each tree had the same number of birds.

Now if you knew how many birds there were in total, then you would know how many trees there were.

What we can tell you is that there was more than one tree, of course to be a wood there must have been, and there were between 400 and 800 birds altogether.

How many birds were there exactly?

There is a hint to solving this puzzle on page 93.

20 After a dreadful start to the season, the village soccer team had a great high scoring victory in the 10th match.

On analysing the results the team coach, who was also something of a statistician, noted that the number of goals scored by the team in the first match indicated the number of times the team had scored just one goal, the score in the second match indicated the number of times the team had scored two goals, the score in the third match indicated the number of times the team had scored three goals, and this carried on right up to the team's score in the 10th match, which indicated the number of times the team had scored zero.

What were the scores for the team in each of the first 10 matches?

21 In the first innings a cricket team scored between 400 and 500 runs. The top four scoring batsmen each scored one-third, one-quarter, one-fifth and one-seventh of the team's total score.

Coincidentally, the sum of the scores of the top four scoring batsmen in the first innings was exactly the total scored by the team in the second innings.

How many did the team score in the first and second innings?

There is a hint to solving this puzzle on page 93.

22 A woman had seven children, including at least one set of triplets. On multiplying their ages together she obtained the number 6591.

Given that today is the birthday of all seven, how many triplets were there, and what are all seven ages?

23

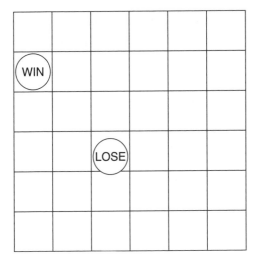

An old fairground game consisted of a sheet of linoleum that had a pattern of 4 inch squares marked out on it.

In order to win a prize a player had to roll a coin down a chute so that the coin rolled onto the linoleum and landed completely within a square and not touching a line.

If the player rolled a 2.5 inch diameter coin down the chute, what are the chances that the coin will fall not touching a line?

24 There is a number that is the cube of a number (that number being less than 25) that is also the sum of four other numbers that are cubes of four successive numbers also less than 25.

Find the numbers.

There is a hint to solving this puzzle on page 93.

25 A space exploration from Earth was being planned for a journey to the planet Mars with an international crew.

A short list for the crew had been drawn up consisting of five European, four American and three Russian astronauts.

Those short-listed were subject to extreme testing as only seven astronauts were required for the trip, plus a leader and a doctor, who were not included in the short list as they had already been selected.

The crew would, therefore, total nine members.

How many possible different teams of nine could be made up from the short-listed astronauts if each team had to include

3 European astronauts
2 American astronauts
2 Russian astronauts

plus the leader and the doctor.

26 In the early 1970s, just after Britain's conversion to decimal coinage, a travelling salesman sent in his expense account, which was rather excessive. His boss asked him 'what is this rather large item?'. 'That's my taxi bill', replied the salesman. 'Well in future don't buy any more taxis', retorted the boss.

Later, when the salesman was being paid his expenses the accountant misread the pounds for the pence and the pence for the pounds.

The man banked the correct amount of the expenses and out of the over-payment purchased a plant for his wife costing £1.52.

The amount that he had remaining from the overpayment was half of the original amount of the expenses.

What was the true expense amount?

27

384	?	96
12	48	192
24	768	6

What is magic about the above square, and what number needs to be produced to complete it?

There is a hint to solving this puzzle on page 93.

28 The two puzzles that follow both involve the same method of solution.

28.1 One man can mow a field in 2 hours
One man can mow a field in 3 hours
One man can mow a field in 4 hours
One man can mow a field in 6 hours.

If they all worked together at their respective speeds, how long would it take to mow the field?

There is a hint to solving this puzzle on page 93.

28.2 The hot tap takes 6 minutes to fill the bath
The cold tap takes 2 minutes to fill the bath
The water empties through the plug-hole in 4 minutes

If both taps are on and the plug is left out, in how many minutes will the bath be filled?

The curiosities

29 What number is missing from the list below?

23, ?, 89, 4567, 78 901, 678 901, 23 456 789, 45 678 901,
9 012 345 678 901, 789 012 345 678 901,
56 789 012 345 678 901 234 567 890 123

30 Divide 987 654 321 by 123 456 789.

What is the answer, which must be correct to seven decimal places?

31 What number is missing?

1, 64, 125, ?, 729, 13 824, 15 625, 117 649, 132 651

There is a hint to solving this puzzle on page 93.

32 Find a four-figure number that is exactly four times greater when the digits are reversed.

33 Explorers discovered the tomb of an ancient mathematician and scholar in an Egyptian pyramid with the number 2520 engraved on the stone lid.

Why was such homage paid to this number?

There is a hint to solving this puzzle on page 93.

34 Le Roi Soleil

Known as the Sun King, because he chose the sun as his royal emblem, Louis XIV (1638–1715) was king of France from 1643 to 1715. His reign, the longest in European history, was marked by a great flowering of French culture.

Louis was born on September 5, 1638. His parents, grateful for a heir after 20 years of marriage, christened him Louis Dieudonné (the gift of God).

The above text reveals a number of numerical curiosities. Can you uncover them?

Section 2
Hints, answers
and explanations

Hints

Chapter 1

19 Jack and Jill must originally have had 80 sweets between them.

41 It is necessary to add the length of the tunnel to the length of the train.

47 Work backwards.

48 Factorial!

Chapter 2

1 The fastest people should make the most crossings and the slowest people the least.

5 How many losers were produced during the tournament?

9 See rules of divisibility in Chapter 4.

13 Use a decimal point.

14 $99 = 72 + 27$, $45 = 27 + 18$, $39 = 18 + 21$. So far so good, so maybe the answer is 15 because $36 = 21 + 15$. However, if this were the case the last number would have to be 8, as $13 + 8 = 21$ and not $13 + 7$. So this cannot be the answer and there has, therefore, to be another (albeit very similar) train of thought that you must apply.

15 It is necessary to think laterally about the additional information that enabled the census taker to know their ages. Obviously it concerns the dog. It cannot concern the fact that the dog has a wooden leg, or is named Tripod, so it must concern the fact that it belongs to the eldest daughter. It is necessary to analyse all the possible three numbers that when multiplied together are equal to 72. You will then see why the additional information is so vital.

Chapter 4

1.2 Add the alternate digits and analyse the result.

1.3 The smallest does not use the digit 9 and the largest does not use the digit 0.

1.4 You may wish to refer to your calculator.

Chapter 5

4 The answer is not 5 mph as many would assume at first sight. Assume the journey is 6 miles each way and calculate the time taken for both the outward jog and the inward walk.

6 What is the sum of the numbers 1–6 inclusive?

7   In order to obtain the smallest fine you must use the ten digits to form the two five-digit numbers closest in value. Your starting point is the numbers 5 and 4.

9   Nineteen trials maximum will determine which door the first key will open, i.e. if she is unlucky enough to try 19 keys in the first door and they all fail, she knows without trying that the 20th key will open the door.

12 Each lady was weighed 4 times. As a starting point add the 10 weights together and divide by 4.

13 If there were one circular path and one path down the centre he would have the choice of 6 (3 × 2) possible routes.

14 How many weights are required to weigh up to and including 7 g?

15 Trays 1−4 together contain 52 + 34 nuts.

Chapter 6

4   There are six possible pairings of the four balls. Write them out and analyse them.

6   Reconsider case 3.

Chapter 7

1   Divide the octagon into eight triangles.

4   Pythagoras.

7 Form a Latin cross.

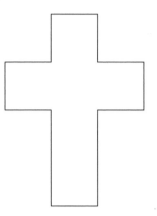

8 Produce four pieces of equal size and shape; however, one of these pieces must then be turned over in order to solve the puzzle.

9 You are looking for two pieces of identical size and shape.

Chapter 8

2 She must enter the last store with £30.00 left.

3 $L - 3 + 6$.

4 Square numbers.

7 Each snail is on the grass for eight snail lengths plus one snail length to get completely off.

11.2 A = 0.

12 1 cu in = 6 sq in area
2 cu in = 9.5256 sq in area.

13    $12 + 4 = 16$ and $6 + 14 = 20$.

16   The key words here are at least. All 100 ladies had at least three items. How many items were there in total?

17   1 is connected to five other numbers.

19.1 The answer must be a prime number to make it unique.

19.2 You are looking for a unique solution, which must be a prime number squared.

21   Factors.

24   Try 20^3.

27   Find the product.

28.1 This puzzle can be solved by using reciprocals, for example, 6 hours would produce the figure $\frac{1}{6}$ or 0.167 and 4 hours would be $\frac{1}{4}$ or 0.25.

31   Cube numbers.

33   Find the factors of 2520.

Answers and explanations

Chapter 1

1   Harry 7, Geoff 5.

2   15.

3   15 handshakes and 30 'Hello's.

    Handshakes:

    $1-2, 1-3, 1-4, 1-5, 1-6, 2-3, 2-4, 2-5, 2-6, 3-4, 3-5, 3-6,$
    $4-5, 4-6, 5-6 = 15$

    or $5 + 4 + 3 + 2 + 1$.

    The number of 'Hello's is twice as many.

4   1 and 13.

5   14 horses and 8 stable hands.

    $14 \times 4 = 56$
    $8 \times 2 = 16$
    22 heads 72 feet.

6   240.

    $1 \times 1 \times 0.5 = 0.5$ cubic metres
    $6 \times 5 \times 4 = 120$ cubic metres

    $120/0.5 = 240$.

7   By one-third. Three of anything, if increased by one-third, becomes four.

8   6.25 kg.

Left hand	Right hand
7 kg × 3 = 21	4 kg × 2 = 8
6 kg × 2 = $\underline{12}$	6.25 kg × 4 = $\underline{25}$
33	33

9   121.

10   45.

11   1425.

$114/8 \times 100$.

12   8.75 days.

The seven men take $7 \times 15 = 105$ man days to build the house. Twelve men can, therefore, build the house in $105/12 = 8.75$ days.

13   35%.

1st stall	8 out of 32	i.e. $\frac{8}{32} = 25\%$
2nd stall	18 out of 30	i.e. $\frac{18}{30} = 60\%$.

14   Peter 32 and Paul 24.

When Peter was 24, Paul was 16 (i.e. half the age Peter is now).

15   10 kg.

$\frac{1}{4}$ of 10 kg = 2.5
$25/2.5 = 10$.

16   Both the same, 80 kg.

$80/4 = 20 + 60 = 80$
$80/5 = 16 + 64 = 80.$

17   10 and 20 metres.

$1000 = 10^2 + 30^2$ i.e. $100 + 900.$

18    $8 + 2 = 10$
$12 - 2 = 10$
$5 \times 2 = 10$
$\dfrac{20/2 = 10}{45}$

19   Jack 50 and Jill 30

	Jack	Jill
	50	30
(i)	20	60
(ii)	40	40
(iii)	0	80

20   Brian 10, Ryan 4

−1	−2	−3			+2
9	8	7	Brian	10	12
3	2	1	Ryan	4	6

21   55 mph.

The next palindromic number after 13931 is 14041. Hannah must have, therefore, travelled 110 miles. As she travelled for 2 hours, her average speed must have been 55 mph.

22   26.

Three numbers $17 \times 3 = 51$
Two numbers $12.5 \times 2 = 25$

The third number must, therefore, be $51 - 25 = 26$.

23   35.

The next cube number below 64 is 27 ($3 \times 3 \times 3$). In order to construct a $3 \times 3 \times 3$ solid cube, therefore, with none left over, $62 - 27 = 35$ blocks need to be taken away.

24   £10.00.

The temptation is to say £20.00 for the cheap watch. This is not correct as £200.00 and £20.00 only represents a difference of £180.00, not £200.00.

The answer is that the cheap watch cost £10.00. The difference between £10 and £210 is, therefore, £200 as stipulated in the question.

25   Apple $= 7$ pence and banana $= 9$ pence.

Multiply the top line by 7 and the bottom line by 6.

Then   42 apples and 28 bananas cost 546 pence
        42 apples and 54 bananas cost 780 pence

subtracting, therefore, 26 ($54 - 28$) bananas cost 234 ($780 - 546$) pence (or 9 pence each)

as six apples and four bananas cost 78 pence, then ($6 \times$ apples) plus (4×9) $= 78$ pence.

So, six apples cost 42 pence ($78 - 36$), and one apple costs 7 pence.

26   £8.00.

starter	= 1 unit	£2.00
sweet	= 2 units	£4.00
main course	= 4 units	£8.00
	$\overline{7}$	$\overline{£14.00}$

The cost per unit = £2.00 ($\frac{14}{7}$).

27   11 am.

If the watch loses 12 minutes per hour it takes 4 hours to lose 48 minutes; i.e., when the correct time is 4 am the watch will show 3.12. As this is the time the watch is now showing it must have stopped at 4 am, therefore the time is now 4 am plus 7 hours = 11 am.

i.e.

12 midnight	= 12 midnight
1 am	= 12.48
2 am	= 1.36
3 am	= 2.24
4 am	= 3.12

plus 7 hours = 11 am.

28   15.6 cm.
(18/7.5) × 6.5.

29   39 lb.

140 less 35% = 91
91 − 26 = 65
65 less $\frac{2}{5}$ (26) = 39.

30   Alice 25, Bill 7, Clara 26, Donald 2, Elsie 5.

31   30.

Although this is probably best solved by trial and error, it can also be solved by algebra as follows:

Let x be my son's age and y my age.

Then five years ago $5(x-5)=(y-5)$

so $5x-25=y-5$

so $5x-20=y$

Today $3x=y$.

Now subtract one from the other, i.e. $2x=20$, therefore x (my son) is 10 today and I am, therefore, 30.

32   The order makes no difference whatsoever. The final price is the original price multiplied by $(\frac{95}{100}) \times (\frac{90}{100}) \times (\frac{80}{100})$ or 68.4% of the original price.

33   You $= 3$, me $= 24$.

Say you $= x$
then me $= 8x$
So, $x + 8x = 3x^2 = 9x$
So $x = 3$.

34   12.36.

12.36 plus 2 minutes $= 12.38$ i.e. 22 minutes before 1 pm.
25 minutes ago it was 12.36 less 25 minutes $= 12.11$.

35   59.

36   110.

Tickets from station 1 to $2-3-4-5-6-7-8-9-10-11 = 10$ tickets.

As above for starting from every station is $10 \times 11 = 110$.

Note that the puzzle asked for the number of single tickets. The number of return tickets is 55.

37   30 minutes.

Formula: $\dfrac{45 \times 8}{12}$

Total time for eight players $= 8 \times 45 = 360$ minutes.

However, as 12 people $(8 + 4)$ are on the pitch for an equal length of time, they are each on the pitch for 30 minutes $(360/12)$.

38   95 guests paid £41.00 each.

39   April has twins of 3 and triplets of 1:
$3 \times 3 \times 1 \times 1 \times 1 = 3 + 3 + 1 + 1 + 1,$

June has triplets of 2 and twins of 1:
$2 \times 2 \times 2 \times 1 \times 1 = 2 + 2 + 2 + 1 + 1.$

40   5, 8, 15.

41   2 minutes 33 seconds.

$(2 + 0.125) \times \dfrac{60}{50}$ or $2.125 \times \dfrac{60}{50}$ or 2.55 minutes

42   23 minutes.

12 noon less 23 minutes $= 11.37$
11.37 less 28 minutes $= 11.09$
10 am plus 69 minutes $(3 \times 23) = 11.09$

Logically 10 am to 12 noon = 120 minutes − 28 = 92
92/4 = 23, i.e. there are three parts after 10 and one part
before 12.

43   404 feet.

44   Yes, but only slightly.

$\frac{5}{16} = 0.3125$

$\frac{25}{81} = 0.3086.$

45   34.5 feet.

12 down	1	12 feet
6 up 6 down	2	12 feet
3 up 3 down	3	6 feet
1.5 up 1.5 down	4	3 feet
0.75 up 0.75 down	5	1.5 feet
		34.5 feet

46   120 different ways ($5 \times 4 \times 3 \times 2 \times 1$).

47   £1.75.

1.75 × 2 = 3.5, less 2 = 1.5, × 2 = 3, less 2 = 1, × 2 = 2,
less 2 = 0.

48   $(4 \times 4!) + 4 = 100.$

4! (factorial) $= 4 \times 3 \times 2 \times 1$ (24)

so $4 \times 24 = 96 + 4 = 100.$

Chapter 2

1   46 minutes.

First Thomas and Sarah cross: 7 minutes.
Then Thomas returns: 5 minutes.
Then Charles and Colonel Chumpkins cross: 20 minutes.
Then Sarah returns: 7 minutes.
Finally Thomas and Sarah cross: 7 minutes.

The fastest people, Thomas and Sarah, therefore make the most crossings (three each) and by sending them across together the two slowest people, Charles and Colonel Chumpkins, only make one crossing each.

2   She knew the cost of the matches and soap, which came to 72 pence.

£2.92 less 72 pence equals £2.20, which is, therefore, what the assistant was charging her for the sugar and pasties. However, £2.20 is not divisible by three, which it would have to be as she was buying nine items of sugar and pasties in total.

3    $1 + 1000 = 1001$
$2 + 999 = 1001$

As there are 500 such pairs the total is $500 \times 1001 = 500\ 500$.

4   986 stripes.

Since 29 is one-third of 87, each fish has the equivalent of 29 stripes after two-thirds of the male fish have been removed. The answer is, therefore, $34 \times 29 = 986$.

Example 1: suppose there were 30 male fish and four female fish. If you took out 20 male fish only, that would leave 10 male fish and four female.

The number of stripes would then be $10 \times 87 = 870$
$$4 \times 29 = 116$$
$$\text{Total} = 986$$

Example 2: if there were 15 male fish and 19 female, and you took out 10 male fish, that would leave five male and 19 female.

The number of stripes would then be $5 \times 87 = 435$
$$19 \times 29 = 551$$
$$\text{Total} = 986$$

In each case the total number of stripes is 986.

5   40 players entered the competition.

In a knock-out tournament, if 39 matches were played there must have been 39 losers. To this it is necessary to add the outright winner i.e. 40 players in total.

6   2.5 miles.

The man walks for 1.5 miles at 3 mph, which takes 30 minutes, or 0.5 hour.

The dog, therefore, runs for 0.5 hour at 5 mph and covers, therefore, 2.5 $\left(\frac{5}{2}\right)$ miles.

7   2.5%.

They must maintain an average of 2.5% increase at all times during the working week, otherwise the weekly average will slip below 2.5%.

8   Zero.

$(x - x)$ will appear in the equation, which will always equal zero.

The answer to the equation is, therefore, zero as every multiplication by zero is always zero.

9   None.

The nine digits add up to 45 and the eight digits add up to 36. As both 45 and 36 are divisible by nine, the number itself will be divisible by nine, in whichever way the digits are arranged.

10   It is impossible. In the first half of the journey I have used up all the time required to achieve 20 mph average.

For example, on a 120 mile journey the first 60 miles at 10 mph would take 6 hours. The second 60 miles at 100 mph would take 1 hour. The 120 miles would take 7 hours, making an average speed of just over 17 mph.

11   5 hours.

In four hours the snail has progressed 4 feet, which leaves 3 feet remaining. In the fifth hour it climbs the remaining 3 feet, and out of the well.

12   Originally Sue had 20 chocolates, Sally had 40, and Stuart had none.

After the deal was made, Sue had 20 (as before), Sally had 20 (20 less than before) and Stuart had 20. Therefore, Sally had contributed 20 and Sue none.

Thus Sally's contribution is 100% and she, therefore, gets 100% of Stuart's £1.00 payment.

13   $\dfrac{9 + 9}{0.9} = 20.$

14   12.

Add up the digits: i.e. $9 + 9 + 7 + 2 = 27$, $4 + 5 + 2 + 7 = 18$ etc., therefore, $3 + 6 + 2 + 1 = 12$.

15   The ages are 3, 3 and 8.

Analyse all the factors of 72. These are as follows:

72	=		added together
		$1 \times 1 \times 72$	$= 74$
		$1 \times 2 \times 36$	$= 39$
		$1 \times 3 \times 24$	$= 28$
		$1 \times 4 \times 18$	$= 23$
		$1 \times 6 \times 12$	$= 19$
		$1 \times 8 \times 9$	$= 18$
		$2 \times 2 \times 18$	$= 22$
		$2 \times 3 \times 12$	$= 17$
		$2 \times 4 \times 9$	$= 15$
		$\mathbf{2 \times 6 \times 6}$	$\mathbf{= 14}$
		$\mathbf{3 \times 3 \times 8}$	$\mathbf{= 14}$
		$3 \times 4 \times 6$	$= 13$

As there are only two sets of numbers that when totalled together equal the same, 14, this must be the Smith's door number, otherwise the census taker would have been able to determine the ages without any additional information. Presumably there must be one set of twins in the household. The information about the eldest daughter enabled the census taker to deduce that the eldest daughter must be 8, and the ages are 3, 3 and 8.

Chapter 3

1.1   280 (8×35).

1.2   14.

1.3

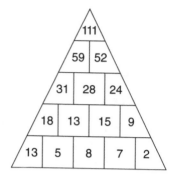

1.4   95.

In another 2 years time we will each be 2 years older, i.e.
$2 \times 3 = 6$ and $89 + 6 = 95$.

1.5   1275 ($250 \times 5 = 1250 + 25 = 1275$).

1.6   £1800.

Sue gets $\frac{3}{5}$ or $\frac{12}{20}$. Les gets 0.35 or $\frac{7}{20}$.
$\frac{12}{20} + \frac{7}{20} = \frac{19}{20}$. Therefore, John must get $\frac{1}{20}$th (£90.00)
£90.00 $\times$ 20 = £1800.

1.7   20.

1.8   38 217.

1.9   280 ($21/12 \times 160$).

1.10 minus £70.00.

$\frac{5}{9}$ of 360	=	200
0.375 of 360	=	135
Cheque	=	95
Total	=	430

1.11 $\frac{1}{2}$ ($\frac{3}{19} \times \frac{38}{12}$ or $\frac{1}{1} \times \frac{2}{4}$).

1.12 Paul 12, Alice 4.

1.13 Total investment £100 000.

Smith 15%   140 000 = 21 000
Jones 30%   140 000 = 42 000
Brown 55% 140 000 = 77 000
                            140 000.

1.14 Harry 42, Barry 56.

Harry $\frac{3}{3}$, Barry $\frac{4}{3}$, i.e. total $\frac{7}{3}$

$98/7 = 14$.

$14 \times 3 = 42$ (Harry), $14 \times 4 = 56$ (Barry).

1.15 7.8 (39/5).

Assessment
14–15   Exceptional
12–13   Very good
9–11   Good
5–8   Average

2.1   39.
      +3, +6, +9 repeated.

2.2   133.
      Add 19 each time.

2.3   127.
      × 2 + 1 each time.

2.4   71.

Less 5.8 each time.

2.5   22.

There are two interwoven series: +2, +4, +8, +16 and +3, +6, +12.

2.6   41.

+7.5, +1, +7.5, +2, +7.5, +3 etc.

2.7   20.

×3, +2 repeated.

2.8   82.5.

−1.5, −2.5, −3.5, −4.5, −5.5.

2.9   17.

+1, +1, +2, +2 etc.

2.10 0.

+3, −4 repeated.

2.11 73.

Minus 6.75 each time.

2.12 15.

There are two interwoven sequences: +2.5 and −2.5.

2.13 24.

×1, ×2, ×3, ×4, ×5, ×6.

2.14 49, 98.

×2, −1 repeated.

2.15 86.

  −8, +2 repeated.

Assessment

14−15   Exceptional
12−13   Very good
9−11   Good
5−8   Average

3.1   9: each adjoining set of three numbers e.g. 14, 5, 2 and 5, 7, 9
       etc., totals 21.

3.2   10: (5 × 8)/4 = 10.

3.3   5147: in all the others the first digit plus the last digit equals the
       number formed by the middle two digits.

3.4   12: (5 × 4) − (9 − 1).

3.5   6: 56 × 6 = 336
       Similarly 43 × 3 = 129 and 87 × 4 = 348.

3.6

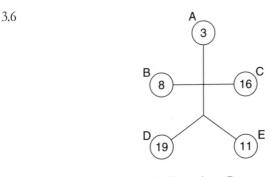

A + B = E; B + E = D; D − A = C.

3.7   120: $(48 \times 5)/2 = 120$.

3.8   114: in each line and column the third and fourth numbers are the sums of the two previous numbers.

3.9   12: $(5 + 8 + 1) - 2$.

3.10   4: $79 \times 6 = 474$.

3.11   3524: in all the others the second digit is the difference between the first and third digits, and the third digit is the difference between the second and fourth digits.

3.12   215: $1 + 1 = 2$ and $8 + 7 = 15$; similarly $3 + 2 = 5$ and $9 + 4 = 13$.

3.13   3: $(7 + 2)/3 = 3$.

3.14   1: in each line and column the middle number is the difference between the first and third numbers.

3.15   13: start at 1 and work clockwise jumping three segments and adding 4 each time.

Assessment
14–15   Exceptional
12–13   Very good
9–11   Good
5–8   Average

4.1   A: lines across are $+3$, lines down are $+4$.

4.2   C: looking across and down the last number in each line and column is the difference between the first two numbers.

4.3   B: looking across the numbers are −1, −2. Looking down they are −2, −1.

4.4   B: in each row and column add the first three numbers to obtain the end number.

4.5   C: looking across the numbers progress +5, −2, +5. Looking down they progress −2, +5, −2.

4.6   B: looking across the numbers progress +1 in the first line, then +2, +3, +4. Looking down they progress +2 in the first column, then +3, +4, +5.

4.7   A: looking across and down each number is the sum of the previous two numbers.

4.8   A: looking across alternate numbers are +1 and +2 respectively. Looking down they are +2, +1.

4.9   C: looking across the numbers progress +4, +3, +2, +1. Looking down they progress +1, +2, +3, +4.

4.10 C: looking across and down the second three numbers are the first three numbers multiplied by 2.

Assessment
9−10   Exceptional
7−8   Very good
5−6   Good
3−4   Average

5.1   56.

5.2   34.

5.3   187.

5.4   105.

5.5   48.

5.6   23.

5.7   75.

5.8   315.

5.9   157.

5.10 134.

5.11 360.

5.12 63.

5.13 290.

5.14 95.

5.15 324.

5.16 249.

5.17 2604.

5.18 45.

5.19 318.

5.20 93.

5.21 2.

5.22 1050.

5.23 846.

5.24 6.25.

5.25 1232.

5.26 702.

5.27 7.

5.28 1.8.

5.29 1725.

5.30 29.

Assessment
28–30   Exceptional
24–27   Very good
17–23   Good
10–16   Average

Chapter 4

1.1

5	3	4	6
2	8	9	3
1	7	8	2
4	2	3	5

1.2 If the difference between the sums of the two sets of alternate digits is any multiple of 11 (for example 11 or 22), then the number is divisible by 11 exactly.

1.3 Smallest: 102 347 586 ($1 + 2 + 4 + 5 + 6 = 0 + 3 + 7 + 8$)
Largest: 987 652 413 ($9 + 7 + 5 + 4 + 3 = 28$;
$8 + 6 + 2 + 1 = 17; 28 - 17 = 11$).

1.4

7	8	9
4	5	6
1	2	3

2 Make sure that the number you write added to the number above it totals 9999. The answer must, therefore, always be $9999 + 9999 + 3144 = 23\ 142$.

3.1 Because the percentages stated in the will do not equal unity, i.e. 1 or 100%.

One-half plus one-quarter plus one-fifth, i.e. $0.5 + 0.25 + 0.2$, only equals 0.95 or 95% ($\frac{19}{20}$).

The will gave the sons an impossible to solve puzzle. It never occurred to the sons that the fractions did not add up to the total inheritance, and so they never bothered to check these figures.

3.2 The question is incorrectly stated. It asserts that each man spent £9.00 plus the £2.00 tip between them; however, the £27.00 *included* the £2.00 tip.

We should say that
the meal cost	£25.00
the waiter's tip	£ 2.00
change	£ 3.00
	£30.00

The question should say that the meal cost £27.00 (including the tip). The total change was £3.00 and as £27.00 + £3.00 equals £30.00, the other £1.00 had not gone anywhere, in fact did not even exist.

4   4100.

If you came up with the answer 5000 this is no cause for concern as this is the total that most people come up with. This is because when adding on the final 20 they jump from four thousand and eighty (4080) to five thousand (5000), when, of course, it should be 4080 + 20 = 4100.

5   Complete the calculations and turn your calculator upside down. The answer to 5.1 (604) reads 'hog' upside down. The answer to 5.2 (71 077.345) reads 'Shell Oil' upside down.

6   Assume the original number chosen is 3 and your age in the year 2003 having already celebrated a birthday is 59.

3
$3 \times 2 = 6$
$6 + 5 = 11$
$11 \times 50 = 550$
$550 + 1753$
$(550 + 1753) - 1944$
$2303 - 1944 = 359$

x

$2x$

$2x + 5$

$100x + 250$

$100x + 2003$

$100x + (2003 - \text{year born})$

In the year 2003, therefore, 2003 less the year born is equal to the current age. $100x +$ current age will produce a three-digit number, i.e. x is a one-digit number and current age a two-digit number (assumed). The first digit of this three-digit number will always be the original number and the second two digits your age, since any time you take 100 times a number and add another two-digit number, the result is the original number followed by the two-digit number added.

The above works in the year 2003. For it to work in subsequent years add 1754 or 1753 in the year 2004, 1755 or 1754 in the year 2005 and so on.

8   The array of numbers is, in effect, an addition table. This table takes the form of two sets of numbers, for example in the array above the sets are 12, 9, 4, 6, 2 and 7, 5, 8, 3 and 10. The sum of all these ten numbers is 66.

As illustrated below, the array is obtained by writing the first set of five numbers horizontally above the top row of the square, and the second set of five numbers vertically alongside the first column. Each number in the array is then calculated by adding the number at the top of the column and the side of the row; for example, the number 19 in the top left hand corner is obtained by adding the numbers 12 and 7, and the number 16 next to it is arrived at by adding the numbers 9 and 7.

	12	9	4	6	2
7	19	16	11	13	9
5	17	14	9	11	7
8	20	17	12	14	10
3	15	12	7	9	5
10	22	19	14	16	12

The way the trick works is that each number in the array represents the sum of a pair of numbers in the two different sets of five numbers. Each of these pairs is eliminated when a circle is drawn round a number in the square. The way the elimination procedure is carried out ensures that eventually the five circled numbers *must* be in different rows and columns. Thus the five circled numbers represent the sums of five *different* pairs of the 10 numbers used to generate the array, which can only be the same as the sum of all 10 numbers.

It is possible to construct a magic square of this kind as large or as small as you like, and with any combination of numbers, positive or negative, integers or fractions. The result will always be the same.

Two further examples are given below in which two sets of integers, 12, 5, 8, 6, 9 and 2, 7, 4, 15, 1 generate a magic 69 in a 5 × 5 array; and two further sets of integers 8, 6, 2, 9 and 14, 12, 1, 3 generate a magic 55 in a 4 × 4 array.

	12	5	8	6	9
2	14	7	10	8	11
7	19	12	15	13	16
4	16	9	12	10	13
15	27	20	23	21	24
1	13	6	9	7	10

	8	6	2	9
14	20	22	16	23
12	20	18	14	21
1	9	7	3	10
3	11	9	5	12

9   Discard the last two digits (which will always be 20) and subtract 3 from the remainder to arrive at the original number.

The mathematics are as follows.

Assume the original number is 7

x	7
$2x$ (double it)	2×7
$2x + 4$ (add 4)	$(2 \times 7) + 4$
$10x + 20$ (multiply by 5)	$5(2 \times 7) + 20$
$10x + 32$ (add 12)	$5(2 \times 7) + 32$
$100x + 320$ (multiply by 10)	$50(2 \times 7) + 320$
	$= 1020$

10   Take the total and cross out the zero at the end. Now subtract 1 and divide by 2.

12.1   Reverse the position of the diagonals:

16	2	3	13
5	11	10	8
9	7	6	12
4	14	15	1

12.2   Read the numbers backwards and it is still a magic square.

Now turn it upside down and the numbers that can now be viewed are also a magic square.

12.3

4	9	8	47	48	49	10
38	19	20	17	34	35	12
39	37	26	27	22	13	11
43	36	21	25	29	14	7
6	18	28	23	24	32	44
5	15	30	33	16	31	45
40	41	42	3	2	1	46

12.4

10	4	13	7
15	5	12	2
8	14	3	9
1	11	6	16

Chapter 5

1

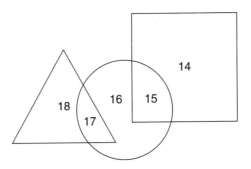

As the numbers are consecutive, the numbers in the triangle must be either 18 and 17 or 17 and 18. As the numbers in the square only total 29, the numbers must be descending left to right, i.e. 18, 17, 16, 15, 14.

2   4 boys and 3 girls.

3   24 minutes.

There are two simple formulas for working out the answer to this puzzle.

(a)   Total time difference, 30 minutes, less time saved, 12 minutes − that is, 18 minutes − plus one-half time saved − that is 6 minutes = 24 minutes.

(b)   Subtract one-half time saved, 6 minutes, from total time difference, 30 minutes = 24 minutes.

It is, however, not necessary to know these formulas as the answer can be worked out by pure logic.

As I leave according to my usual schedule, we know it is before 17.30 when I pick up my wife. Because we have saved 12 minutes, that must be the same time that it takes me to drive from the point I picked her up, to the station, and back to that same point. Assuming it takes an equal 6 minutes each way, I have, therefore, picked up my wife 6 minutes before I would normally do so, which means 17.24. So my wife must have walked from 17.00 to 17.24, or for 24 minutes.

4   4.8 mph.

Let us say, for ease of calculation, that the journey was 6 miles each way. Then at 6 mph the outward jog would take 1 hour and the inward walk 1.5 hours ($4/6 \times 60 = 1.5 \times 60 = 90$ minutes).

This means that it takes 2.5 hours to travel 12 miles, or 1 hour to travel 4.8 miles (12/2.5).

5   8 pm.

As the faster watch gains on the slower one by 3 minutes per hour, it will be exactly 1 hour ahead after 20 hours ($20 \times 3 = 60$).

6   5 1 3 6 2 4 (or 4 2 6 3 1 5).

As the sum of the numbers 1–6 is 21, the numbers 5 and 4 must be in the two end circles.

The numbers 5 and 6 must have numbers totalling 4 between them. As 4 is already placed these numbers must be 3 and 1 or 1 and 3.
This leaves 2, which must be placed in the only remaining space next to the 4 at the end, from which it can be determined that 1 must be placed next to 5 at the end.

7   247 Euros.

50 123 − 49 876. These are the two closest possible numbers in value using the digits 0–9 only once each.

8   39.

This puzzle can be solved by trial and error or by algebra; however, a more intuitive and elegant method is, in our opinion, to solve it by logical analysis.

If the average was raised by 1 by scoring 8 over the average, then it will be raised by a further 1 for each extra 8. This means a total of 8 innings already.

So, to increase the average by 3 instead of 1, add 24 instead of 8 to the original average of 15, to get 39.

9   190.

19 + 18 + 17 + 16 + 15 + 14 + 13 + 12 + 11 + 10 + 9 + 8 + 7 + 6 + 5 + 4 + 3 + 2 + 1.

A formula that emerges from this analysis is number of rooms less 1 multiplied by half the number of rooms.

In this case:

number of rooms 20 − 1	=	19
× $\frac{1}{2}$ number of rooms	=	10
		190

10   40.

If he takes out 38 socks, although it is a long shot, they could be all the blue and all the red. To make sure he also has a pair of black he must take out two more socks.

11   The second option.

First option (£1000.00 increase after each 12 months)

First year	£15 000 + £15 000 = £30 000
Second year	£15 500 + £15 500 = £31 000

Second option (£250.00 increase after 6 months)

First year	£15 000 + £15 250 = £30 250
Second year	£15 500 + £15 750 = £31 250.

12   As each lady was weighed four times (for example A with B, C, D and E), it is necessary to first of all add the 10 weights together (1156 kg) and divide by 4 to give the total weight of the five ladies (289 kg).

If the ladies are called Mrs A, Mrs B, Mrs C, Mrs D and Mrs E, in ascending order of weight A + B must weigh 110 kg and D + E must weigh 121 kg, therefore, C weighs 289 − (110 + 121) = 58 kg.

From this it is possible to determine the other weights, i.e. A + C = 112, therefore A = 54 kg; A + B = 110 kg, therefore B = 56; A + D = 113, therefore D = 59 kg, and D + E = 121, therefore E = 62 kg.

13   216 different routes.

If there were only one circular path the man could continue in three ways when first reaching the intersection (left, right or straight forward). On reaching the second intersection he would have the choice of just two routes, as he could not go back the same way he had just come, so that altogether there would be six (3×2) possible routes, 6^1. If the number of circular routes were increased to two the choice of routes would be increased to 36 (6^2). We thus see a pattern emerging and with four circular paths the choice of routes is 6^4, or 216 ($6 \times 6 \times 6 \times 6$).

This formula is valid for any number of circular routes.

14    $1-2-4-8-16-32-64-128$.

Two weights of 1 g and 2 g will enable you to weigh up to and including 3 g. To weigh an object of 4 g another weight is required. The best result is by taking a weight of 4 g so that you can weigh up to 7 g.

To continue, we need another weight of $7 + 1 = 8$ g as this gives combinations up to and including 15 g. By continuing in this way we see a sequence emerging, and for the eight weights obtain the set $1-2-4-8-16-32-64-128$.

15   Tray 1 = 27, tray 2 = 25, tray 3 = 18, tray 4 = 16 and tray 5 = 14.

Trays $1 + 2 + 3 + 4 = 86$ ($1 + 2 = 52$ and $3 + 4 = 34$)
so   tray 5 $= 100 - 86 = 14$
and   tray 4, therefore, $= 30 - 14 = 16$
       tray 3 + 4 $= 34$ and as tray 4 is 16, tray 3 must be 18
       tray 2 + 3 $= 43$ and as tray 3 is 18, tray 2 must be 25
       tray 1 + 2 $= 52$ and as tray 2 is 25, tray 1 must be 27.

Chapter 6

1   1 in 16, or 15–1.

Each car is red or blue, i.e. 1 in 2.

To repeat five times is 2 to the power 5, or

$2 \times 2 \times 2 \times 2 \times 2 = 32$.

However, as the first car must either be red or blue, the first car does not come into the calculation.

The answer is, therefore 2 to the power 4, or

$2 \times 2 \times 2 \times 2 = 16$, or $\frac{15}{1}$.

2   In a pack of 52 cards there are 32 cards of nine or below. The chance that the first card dealt is one of the 32 is $\frac{32}{52}$, the second card $\frac{31}{51}$ etc.

The chance of all 13 being favourable is $\frac{32}{52} \times \frac{31}{51}$ ... $\frac{20}{40}$, or $\frac{1}{1828}$.

The odds were, therefore, strongly in Earl Yarborough's favour.

3   9.

Tabulate the possibilities as follows:

1–1	1–2	1–3	1–4	1–5	1–6
2–1	2–2	2–3	2–4	2–5	2–6
3–1	3–2	3–3	3–4	3–5	**3–6**
4–1	4–2	4–3	4–4	**4–5**	**4–6**
5–1	5–2	5–3	**5–4**	**5–5**	5–6
6–1	6–2	**6–3**	**6–4**	6–5	6–6

9 is possible on four throws

10 is only possible on three throws.

4   One in five.

There are six possible pairings of the four balls:

red/red   red 2/white
red 1/white   red 2/black
red 1/black   white/black

We can eliminate the white/black combination, which leaves five other possible combinations. The chances that the red/red combination has been drawn out is, therefore, one in five.

5   Three chances in eight.

There are 32 (2^5) different ways for the coins to fall, as the first coin may fall either heads or tails, as may the second, third, fourth and fifth coins.

If the 32 different ways are analysed the results can be summarized as follows.

1. Five heads (one way) HHHHH
2. Five tails (one way)
3. Four heads and one tail (five ways) THHHH, HTHHH, HHTHH, HHHTH, HHHHT
4. Four tails and one head (five ways)
5. Three heads and two tails (10 ways) HHHTT, HHTTH, HTTHH, HHTTT, THHHT, THHTH, THTHH, HTHTT, HTHHT, HHTHT
6. Three tails and two heads (10 ways).

Of these, 1, 2, 3 and 4 (12 ways) are favourable, but the other 20 ways, 5 and 6, are not. The chances, therefore, are 12 chances out of 32, or three chances out of eight.

6   No, his reasoning was incorrect. D'Alembert made the error of not carrying through his analysis far enough. The three cases are not equally likely, and the only way to obtain equally likely cases is, in the third case, to toss the coin again even when the first toss is heads, so that the third case has, in fact, two options and becomes the third and fourth cases. The four possible cases are, therefore, as follows.

(a) Tails appears on the first toss and again on the second toss
(b) Tails appears on the first toss and heads on the second toss

(c) Heads appears on the first toss and again on the second toss

(d) Heads appears on the first toss and tails on the second.

As there are now proved to be four cases, and as three of these are favourable, then the possibility of heads at least once is, in fact, $\frac{3}{4}$.

7   Three chances in four.

The possible combinations of drawing the balls are

odd – odd
odd – even
even – odd
even – even.

There is only one of these combinations where an odd numbered ball is not drawn out (the even – even combination). The chances of drawing at least one odd numbered ball are, therefore, three in four.

8   The chances of a pair of black socks were nil.

He must have had three white socks and one black sock in his drawer.

The combinations for three white socks and one black sock are

W1 – W2
W2 – W3
W1 – W3.

The other combinations are

W1 – B
W2 – B
W3 – B

so half of these, or $\frac{50}{50}$, are correct as three out of six possible combinations are favourable.

If he had two white socks and two black socks in the drawer then the possible combinations would be

W1–W2
B1–B2
W1–B1
W1–B2
W2–B1
W2–B2.

The chances of a pair of white, therefore would have only been one in six.

Chapter 7

1   135°.

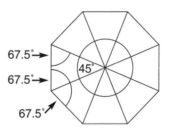

All circles have a value of 360°; therefore, each segment created by the circle and triangles inside the octagon is 45°, as shown above, or 360/8.

As all triangles have a value of 180°, the sum of the other two angles in each of the triangles in the figure above must be $180 - 45 = 135°$. The other two angles, being equal, must, therefore, each be $135/2 = 67.5°$.

The total value of each internal angle is, therefore $67.5 \times 2 = 135°$.

2   At first glance it appears to be a right-angled triangle (90°), but it is not. If a third diagonal is drawn, line AC, an equilateral triangle is created. The answer is, therefore, 60°.

The three internal angles of a triangle always add up to 180°; therefore, in an equilateral triangle each angle is $180°/3 = 60°$.

3   46: 28 edges and 18 faces.

4   12 cm.

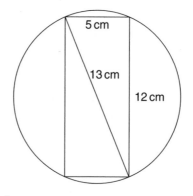

$$13^2 = 12^2 + 5^2$$

5   They never will. In a heptagon, three places clockwise is the same as four places anti-clockwise. The arrow and star will always keep two places between them, and in seven stages will have returned to their original starting positions.

6.1

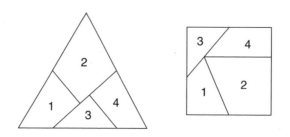

6.2

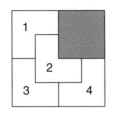

6.3

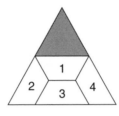

7

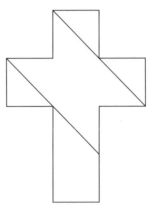

8

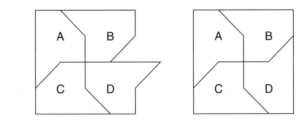

Piece D is turned over.

9

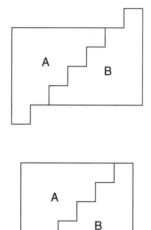

Chapter 8

1   8694.

2   £450.00.

Start at the last store, in which she spends her last £10.00 in the last half hour. She must, therefore, have had £30.00 when she entered, i.e. she spends £10.00 in the first half hour, half the money left in the second half hour (20/2) and £10.00 in the last half hour.

Now work this back throughout all four stores:

Enters 4th store with £30.00   10   10   10   (30 − 30 = 0)
Enters 3rd store with £90.00   10   40   10   (90 − 60 = 30)
Enters 2nd store with £210.00   10   100   10   (210 − 120 = 90)
Enters 1st store with **£450.00**   10   220   10   (450 − 240 = 210).

3   Jim painted 6 metres more than Sid.

Call the length of the street L metres.

Jim painted $L - 3 + 6 = L + 3$ metres and Sid painted $3 + L - 6 = L - 3$ metres.

Therefore, Jim painted 6 metres more than Sid. The length of the street is irrelevant.

4   3025.

The sequence comprises the squares of successive Kaprekar numbers. A Kaprekar number is one which, when it is squared and when the result is divided into two sets of digits – one to the left and one to the right – produces numbers that can be added to give the original square root.

For example, $55^2 = 3025$ and $30 + 25 = 55$.

Similarly $99^2 = 9801$ and $98 + 01 = 99$

and $2223^2 = 4\ 941\ 729$ and $494 + 1729 = 2223$.

5   Add $46\ 298 + 2648 + 5216 + 7141 + 10\ 692 = 71\ 995$. Now divide by $5 = 14\ 399$.

14 399 is the number of votes received by the successful candidate.

The second received $14\ 399 - 2648 = 11\ 751$
The third received $14\ 399 - 5216 = 9183$
The fourth received $14\ 399 - 7141 = 7258$
The fifth received $14\ 399 - 10\ 692 = 3707$.

6   381 654 729.

7   Answer:

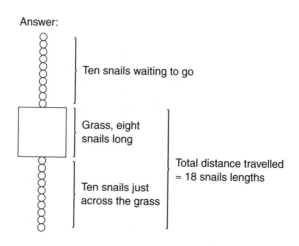

First snail

Each snail is on the grass
for eight snail lengths, plus
one snail length to get off.

18 snail lengths in 50 minutes.
Speed is 50/18 snail lengths per minute. Therefore, time on
grass for each snail equals $9 \times 50/18 = 25$ minutes.

8.1   301.

$301/2 = 150 + 1$ over; $301/3 = 100 + 1$ over; $301/4 = 75 + 1$
over; $301/5 = 60 + 1$ over; $301/6 = 50 + 1$ over; $301/7 = 43$.

8.2   2519.

$2519/3 = 839$ tables $+ 2$ guests left over
$2519/5 = 503 + 4$ over
$2519/7 = 359 + 6$ over
$2519/9 = 279 + 8$ over
$2519/11 = 229$ exactly.

9

4	÷	2	+	7	=	9
×		+		+		−
6	+	4	−	7	=	3
÷		×		−		÷
8	−	2	−	5	=	1
=		=		=		=
3	+	12	−	9	=	6

10   Cancel out the two common digits top and bottom and the value is the same:

$$\frac{1}{4} \qquad \frac{1}{5} \qquad \frac{2}{5}$$

11.1 $1 + 2 + 3 + 4 + 567 + 89 = 666$
$123 + 456 + 78 + 9 = 666$
$9 + 87 + 6 + 543 + 21 = 666$

11.2
$$
\begin{array}{r}
487 \\
487 \\
487 \\
39\ 045 \\
\hline
40\ 506
\end{array}
$$

12   He would actually pay slightly less!

1 inch square (for example) = 1 cu in volume, or 6 sq in area.
1.26 inch square cube = 2 cu in volume or 9.5256 sq in area.

Similarly 5 inch square = 125 cu in volume or 150 sq in area.
6.3 inch square = 250 cu in volume or 238 sq in area.

To double the volume would require approximately 58.75% increase in cardboard, i.e. the percentage increase from 6 to 9.5256.

For every £100.00 worth of cardboard he would have to pay £158.75, but the discount of 37.5% on the new figure reduces this to £99.22.

13    $12 \dfrac{3576}{894} = 16$

$6 \dfrac{13\ 258}{947} = 20$

14   47.5
         386.27
           1.254
        $\underline{15.833}$
         450.857

15

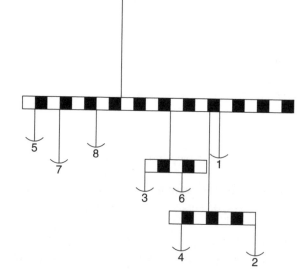

left-hand side	right-hand side
$7 \times 5 = 35$	$7 \times 6 (4 + 2) = 42$
$5 \times 7 = 35$	$4 \times 9 (3 + 6) = 36$
$2 \times 8 = \underline{16}$	$1 \times 8 \qquad = \underline{8}$
86	86

16   Add the items together, i.e. $85 + 75 + 60 + 90 = 310$

Each of the 100 ladies had at least three items (300), therefore, 10 ladies $(310 - 300)$ must have had four items at least.

17

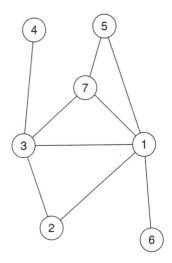

18   The actual chances are 54 in 100.

The calculation is $\frac{364}{365} \times \frac{363}{365} \times \frac{362}{365} \times \frac{361}{365} \cdots \frac{342}{365} = \frac{46}{100}$.

This figure is the probability that there will be no two people sharing the same birthday. The probability, therefore, that two people at least will match is $\frac{54}{100}$.

19.1   17 aliens with 17 fingers each.

First consider numbers between 200 and 300 that have different factors. That could be

	20 aliens with 12 fingers
or	12 aliens with 20 fingers
or	10 aliens with 24 fingers
or	24 aliens with 10 fingers.

However, this is not unique, so all numbers that have different factors must be eliminated.

Next try prime numbers (a prime number is a number that has no factors except 1 and itself, for example 233) So that could be one alien with 233 fingers (but there is more than 1 alien) or 233 aliens with one finger each (but each alien has more than one finger).

This is also not a unique answer, so all prime numbers in the range are eliminated.

That leaves only the square of a prime number. There is only one between 200 and 300, which is 289, the square of 17.

The answer, therefore, can only be 17 aliens each with 17 fingers.

19.2   Between 400 and 800 there is only one prime number squared, which is 529, the square of 23 (a prime number).

Therefore, there are 23 trees each with 23 birds.

20   2 1 0 0 0 1 0 0 0 6.

21   420 first innings ($3 \times 4 \times 5 \times 7$). 389 in the second innings, i.e. the sum of each factor of 420: $140 + 105 + 84 + 60$.

22   1, 1, 1, 3, 13, 13, 13.

Since today is all of their birthdays, their ages are all integers.
So there must be seven integers that multiply together to make
6591. If you take the prime factorization of 6591, you get
3 × 13 × 13 × 13. Having one year old triplets won't change
the product of their ages, so you end up with seven kids: a set
of one year old triplets, a three year old, and a set of 13 year old
triplets.

23   For a coin to fall within a square, its centre must fall within the
shaded area as illustrated below.

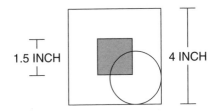

If it falls outside it will touch a line.

The chances are

Successful   1.5 × 1.5 = 2.25
Unsuccessful   16 (4 × 4) − 2.25 = 13.75

The odds, therefore, are 13.75 to 2.25 or (multiplied by 4 to get
to round figures): 55 to 9 against.

24   8000 = 20 × 20 × 20.

11 × 11 × 11   =   1331
12 × 12 × 12   =   1728
13 × 13 × 13   =   2197
14 × 14 × 14   =   2744
                        ─────
                         8000

25   720 different possible combinations.

As two out of the nine were to be included in every team, it is only necessary to consider seven out of the 12 available.

	European		American		Russian
	$\dfrac{5 \times 4 \times 3 \times 2 \times 1}{3 \times 2 \times 1}$	$\times$	$\dfrac{4 \times 3 \times 2 \times 1}{2 \times 1}$	$\times$	$\dfrac{3 \times 2 \times 1}{2 \times 1}$
=	20	$\times$	12	$\times$	3
=	720				

26   original   36.56
      reversed   56.36
      profit   19.80
      plant   1.52
      remainder   18.28.

27   3.

The product of each row, column and corner-to-corner line is the same: 110 592.

28.1 48 minutes.

Suppose one man takes 2 hours to mow a cricket pitch. Now suppose another man helps him, who also takes 2 hours, then together they will obviously mow the pitch in one hour, or half the time, or $1/2 + 1/2 = 1$ (or $0.5 + 0.5$). If the task individually took each man 4 hours, then they would take 2 hours working together. Using the same calculation process as above, $1/4 + 1/4 = 1/2$ (or $0.25 + 0.25 = 0.5$), however, as 0.5 does not give the actual time taken, it is necessary to divide this into 1, i.e. $1/0.5$, to arrive at the actual time taken of 2 hours.

This figure is known as a reciprocal, which in this definition is the quotient resulting from dividing unity (1) by a quantity. For example, the reciprocal of 4 is $1/4 = 0.25$ and the reciprocal of 2.5 is $1/2.5 = 0.4$.

This method can, therefore, be applied to much more complicated problems. Let us imagine, for example, that one man takes 2 hours to mow a field, and the other takes 3 hours. Then, unlike the examples given above, it is not so easy to arrive at the correct answer with a quick piece of mental arithmetic, as it is not correct to say that when they work together they complete the work in $2 + 3 = 5$ hours divided by 2 (2.5 hours), because the faster worker will also do more work than the other.

To arrive at the correct answer, therefore, it is necessary to apply the same method using reciprocals as in the earlier examples.

Thus   man A takes 2 hours $= 1/2 = 0.5$
man B takes 3 hours $= 1/3 = 0.333$
total 0.833

and $1/0.833 = 1.20$ hours, or 1 hour 12 minutes.

Applying the same process the answer to this puzzle is, therefore, as follows:

man A	2 hours	1/2	=	0.5
man B	3 hours	1/3	=	0.333
man C	4 hours	1/4	=	0.25
man D	6 hours	1/6	=	0.167
			total	1.25

Taking the reciprocal again, then $1/1.25 = 0.8$ hours, or 48 minutes.

28.2   2 minutes 24 seconds.

The same reasoning applies here as in the answer to puzzle 28.1.

$1/6 + 1/2 - 1/4 = 0.416.$

hot tap	1/6	=	0.166
cold tap	1/2	=	0.5
add			0.666
plug empties	1/4	=	0.25
deduct			0.416

Taking the reciprocal again, the bath fills in $1/0.416$ minutes, or 2 minutes 24 seconds.

29   67.

It is a list of prime numbers of two digits or more, where all digits are consecutive.

30   8.000 000 0. To ten decimal places the answer is 8.000 000 072 9.

31   216: it is a list of cube numbers where the final digit or the final two digits is the cube root, i.e. $6 \times 6 \times 6 = 216$.

32   2178.

33   2520 is the lowest number into which all the numbers from 1 to 9 inclusive will divide without remainder.

34   Louis XIV = Louis 14th, and the number 14 appears over and over again in the King's life.

1643 (year came to throne): total of digits 14
1715 (year of death): total of digits 14
September fifth (date of birth) = 14 letters

September (9th month) + fifth (5) = 14
Louis Dieudonné (birth name) = 14 letters.

His year of birth, 1638, does not total 14; however, if you add 1638 to the year of his death (1715) you arrive at the total 3353, the digits of which do total 14.

Section 3
Glossary and data

Glossary

Whilst it is impossible to include a list of every mathematical term in this book, as such a list would far exceed the space available, nevertheless the following are a selection of common and not so common mathematical terms that it is considered might prove of use or interest.

Algebra
A branch of mathematics in which letters are used to represent basic arithmetic relations.

Aliquot part
A part that is a division of the whole without remainder.

Arabic system
The common system of number notation, 1, 2, 3, 4, 5, ..., in use in most parts of the world today. The system was first developed by the Hindus and was in use in India in the third century BC. At that time the numerals 1, 4 and 6 were written in much the same form as they are today. The Hindu numeral system was probably introduced into the Arab world in about the seventh or eighth century AD. The first recorded use of the system in Europe was in 976.

Area
In mathematics, the size of an enclosed region given in terms of the square of a designated unit of length.

Arithmetic
Literally, the art of counting.

Automorphic number
A square number that ends in the same two digits as its square root, for example $76^2 = 5776$.

Binary
The number system used in computer science, using only the two integers 0 and 1.

Cube number
A number multiplied by itself twice, for example $2 \times 2 \times 2$ (8) is written 2^3 and is called two cubed.

Decimal system
A system of numbers based on 10 or the powers of 10.

Degree
An arc equalling $\frac{1}{360}$ of the circumference of a circle.

Dodecahedron
A solid figure with 12 faces.

Duodecimal
A number system using a base of 12.

Equality
In mathematics, the symbol of equality consisting of two little parallel lines, =, was originated by the English mathematician Robert Recorde (c. 1510–58). He is reputed to have said *nothing is more equal than parallel lines*.

Equation
Statement of an equality between two expressions.

Factorial

Sometimes referred to in olden times as shriek because it is denoted by an exclamation mark (!). For example, $4! = 4 \times 3 \times 2 \times 1 = 24$.

Fibonacci sequence

The number sequence 0, 1, 1, 2, 3, 5, 8, 13, 21, 34, 55, 89 where each number is the sum of the previous two.

(See Appendix 1.)

Geometry

(Greek *geo-*, earth; *metrein*, to measure), a branch of mathematics that deals with the properties of space.

Heptagonal numbers

Arranged heptagonal points around a central plane, the first three heptagonal numbers being 1, 7, 18 as illustrated below:

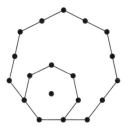

Hexagonal numbers

Arranged hexagonal points around a central plane, the first three hexagonal numbers being 1, 6, 13 as illustrated below:

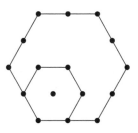

Hexominoes

Tiles formed by six squares arranged edge to edge, for example

Hexadecimal

A number system to a base of 16 used in computer science. To the usual numbers $0-9$, the letters $A-F$ are added.

Icosahedron

A solid figure with 20 faces.

Magic square

An array of consecutive numbers in which each row and column, and the two main diagonals, add up to the same number.

Mersenne numbers

Integers in the form $M_n = 2^n - 1$. Named after the French mathematician and monk Marin Mersenne (1588–1648). The fifth Mersenne number is $31 = 2^n - 1$.

Natural numbers

The simplest numbers 1, 2, 3, ... used in counting, also called *whole numbers, positive integers or positive rational integers.*

Octagonal numbers

Arranged octagonal points around a central point, the first three octagonal numbers being 1, 8 and 21 as illustrated below:

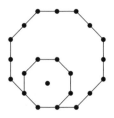

Palindromic numbers
Numbers that read the same in reverse, for example 121. In temperature 28 °C is known as the *palindromic 82* because it is equal to 82 °F.

Parallelogram
A four-sided figure (quadrilateral) in which each side is equal in length to its opposite side, and the opposite sides parallel to each other.

Pentagonal numbers
Arranged pentagonal points around a central point, for example, the first three pentagonal numbers are 1, 5 and 10 as illustrated below:

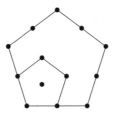

Percentage
Latin per centum, meaning per hundred. The fraction of a whole number expressed in hundredths.

Perfect number
A number that is equal to the sum of its aliquot parts, that is, its own divisors but not itself. For example the number 6 is perfect because its divisors, 1, 2 and 3, total 6.

Pi
The Greek letter (π) used in mathematics as the symbol for the ratio of a circle to its diameter. Its value is approximately 22/7 or 3.141 59. *(See Appendix 2.)*

Polygon
A closed plane figure formed by the joining of three or more straight lines.

Prime number
A number greater than 1, which has no factors other than 1 and itself. 1 is not considered to be a prime number, the first seven prime numbers being 2, 3, 5, 7, 11, 13 and 17. The largest prime number below 5000 is 4999 and the largest below 10 000 is 9973.

Product
The result of multiplying two numbers together.

Pyramidal numbers
The sequence produced by arranging numbers in a pyramid shape, for example the numbers that would be produced by each new layer of cannonballs stacked on a square base.

Quotient
A number resulting from division.

Rational numbers
In mathematics, a class of numbers that can be expressed as a quotient of two integers.

Reciprocal
The result of dividing a number into 1, for example, the reciprocal of 16 is 0.0625 (1/16).

Rectangle
A four-sided figure in which only opposite sides are equal in length, and sides meet at right angles.

Rhombus
A four-sided figure in which all sides are equal in length, but do not meet at right angles.

Sexadecimal
A system of numbering using a base of 60.

Sidereal year
The time required for one complete revolution of the earth about the sun relative to the fixed stars, or 365 days, 6 hours, 9 minutes, 9.54 seconds in units of mean solar time.

Solar year
The period of time required for the earth to make one complete revolution around the sun, measured from one vernal equinox to the next and equal to 365 days, 5 hours, 38 minutes, 45.51 seconds. Also called *astronomical year*, *tropical year.*

Square number
A number multiplied by itself, for example 4×4 (16) is written 4^2 and called four squared.

Sum
The result of adding numbers together.

Tetrahedral
An arrangement, for example, of cannonballs stacked solidly in layers on a triangular base.

Topology
A term that deals with those properties of geometric figures that remain unaltered when the space they inhabit is bent, twisted, stretched or deformed in any way.
(See Appendix 3.)

Triangular numbers
Numbers arranged in triangular form in one layer, the first four triangular numbers being, 1, 3, 6 and 10 as illustrated below.

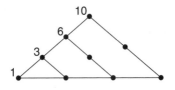

Data

He uses statistics as a drunken man uses a lamppost – for support rather than for illumination.

Andrew Lang

As with the glossary, we could fill a whole book with the plethora of tables and data that is available. We have, therefore, chosen just a short selection of data that we believe may prove particularly useful or interesting.

Units of conversion

Linear measure

1 mil	0.001 inch	0.0254 millimetres
1 inch	1000 mils	2.54 centimetres
12 inches	1 foot	0.3048 metre
3 feet	1 yard	0.9144 metre
1 mile	5280 feet	1.6094 kilometres
	1 millimetre	0.039 37 inch
10 millimetres	1 centimetre	0.3937 inch
10 centimetres	1 decimetre	3.937 inches
10 decimetres	1 metre	39.37 inches or 3.2808 feet
10 metres	1 decimetre	393.7 inches or 32.8083 feet
10 decimetres	1 hectometre	328.083 feet
10 hectometres	1 kilometre	0.621 mile or 3280.83 feet
10 kilometres	1 myriametre	6.21 miles

Square measure

	1 square inch	6.452 square centimetres
144 square inches	1 square foot	929.03 square centimetres
9 square feet	1 square yard	0.8361 square metres
1 acre	4840 square yards	43 560 square feet
640 acres	1 square mile	259 hectares
	1 square millimetre	0.001 55 square inch
100 square millimetre	1 square centimetre	0.154 99 square inch
100 square centimetre	1 square decimetre	15.499 square inch
100 square decimetre	1 square metre	1549.9 square inch
100 square metres	1 square decimetre	119.6 square yards
1 square metre	1 centiare	1549.9 square inch
100 square decimetre	1 square hectometre	2.471 acres
100 centiares	1 are	119.6 square yards
100 ares	1 hectare	2.471 acres
100 hectometres	1 square kilometre	0.386 square mile
100 hectares	0.386 square mile	247.1 acres

Cubic measure

	1 cubic inch	16.387 cubic centimetres
1728 cubic inches	1 cubic foot	0.0283 cubic metre
16 cubic feet	1 cord foot	0.453 cubic metres
128 cubic feet	1 cord	3.625 cubic metres
27 cubic feet	1 cubic yard	0.7646 cubic metres
1000 cubic millimetres	1 cubic centimetre	0.06102 cubic inch
1000 cubic centimetre	1 cubic decimetre	61.023 cubic inches
1000 cubic decimetres	1 cubic metre	35.314 cubic feet

Pythagorean numbers (1–100)

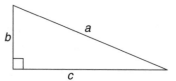

$$a^2 = b^2 + c^2$$

b	c	a	b	c	a
3	4	5	25	60	65
5	12	13	27	36	45
6	8	10	28	45	53
7	24	25	28	96	100
8	15	17	30	40	50
9	12	15	30	72	78
9	40	41	32	60	68
10	24	26	33	44	55
11	60	61	33	56	65
12	16	20	35	84	91
12	35	37	36	48	60
13	84	85	36	77	85
14	48	50	39	52	65
15	20	25	39	80	89
15	36	39	40	42	58
16	30	34	40	75	85
16	63	65	42	56	70
18	24	30	45	60	75
18	80	82	48	55	73
20	21	29	48	64	80
20	48	52	51	68	85
21	28	35	54	72	90
21	72	75	57	76	95
24	32	40	60	63	87
24	45	51	60	80	100
24	70	74	65	72	97

Prime numbers up to 1000

2	3	5	7	11	13	17	19
23	29	31	37	41	43	47	53
59	61	67	71	73	79	83	89
97	101	103	107	109	113	127	131
137	139	149	151	157	163	167	173
179	181	191	193	197	199	211	223
227	229	233	239	241	251	257	263
269	271	277	281	283	293	307	311
313	317	331	337	347	349	353	359
367	373	379	383	389	397	401	409
419	421	431	433	439	443	449	457
461	463	467	479	487	491	499	503
509	521	523	541	547	557	563	569
571	577	587	593	599	601	607	613
617	619	631	641	643	647	653	659
661	673	677	683	691	701	709	719
727	733	739	743	751	757	761	769
773	787	797	809	811	821	823	827
829	839	853	857	859	863	877	881
883	887	907	911	919	929	937	941
947	953	967	971	977	983	991	997

Section 4
Appendices

Appendix 1

Fibonacci and nature's use of space

The Fibonacci series

0, 1, 1, 2, 3, 5, 8, 13, 21, 34, 55, 89, 144, 233, 377, 610, 987, 1597, ...

Referred to as the *greatest European mathematician of the middle ages*, Leonardo of Pisa, or Leonardo Pisano in Italian, was born in Pisa, Italy, about AD 1175. Leonardo's father, Guglielmo Bonaccio, was a customs officer in the North African town of Bugia (now Bougie), so Leonardo grew up with a North African education under the Moors. He later travelled extensively round the Mediterranean coast, meeting many merchants and learning of their system of arithmetic, quickly realizing the many advantages of the Hindu–Arabic system over all the others.

Although his correct name is Leonardo of Pisa, he called himself Fibonacci, short for *filus Bonacci*, or *son of Bonacci*.

Fibonacci was one of the first people to introduce the Hindu–Arabic number system into Europe. His book *Liber Abbaci*, meaning *Book of the Abacus*, or *Book of Calculating*, completed in 1202, persuaded many European mathematicians of his day to use the new system.

In *Liber Abbaci*, Fibonacci introduced the following problem for readers to use to practice their arithmetic.

Suppose a newly born pair of rabbits, one male, one female, is put in a field. The rabbits mate at the end of one month so that at the end of its second month a female can produce another pair of rabbits. It must be assumed that the rabbits never die, nor do any escape from the field, and that the female always produces one new pair (one male, and one female) every month, without fail, from the second month on.

How many pairs of rabbits will there be in any one year?

The puzzle is solved as follows.

1. At the end of the first month the rabbits mate, but there is still only one pair.

2. After month two the female produces another pair, which means there are now two pairs of rabbits in the field.

3. After the third month, the original female produces another pair, so that there are now three pairs in the field.

4. At the end of the fourth month, the original female has produced another new pair, whilst the female born two months ago has also produced her first pair, making five pairs in total.

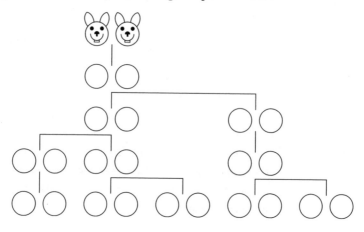

Already we can see a pattern emerging. The monthly totals up to now are 1, 1, 2, 3, 5; in other words, each third number is the sum of the previous two numbers, and the Fibonacci sequence is born, and continues 1, 1, 2, 3, 5, 8, 13, 21, ... etc.

However, it was not until the 19th century that the French mathematician Eduard Lucus gave the name Fibonacci to this series and found many important applications for it.

The Fibonacci series occurs often in the natural world and one such example, the construction of shell spirals (the nautilus), is demonstrated below.

Start by drawing two small squares, each with sides of one unit.

Next draw another square with sides of two units with one border common to the two one unit squares, then another having sides of three units, then another of five units then eight and finally 13.

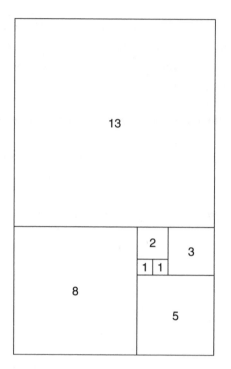

It is possible to continue adding squares ad infinitum, each new square having a side that is as long as the previous two squares' sides.

By constructing rectangles comprised of squares in this way we can see the Fibonacci sequence reveal itself, 1, 1, 2, 3, 5, 8, 13.

Next draw a spiral by drawing quarter circles in each square with their centres in the opposite corner of each square to the arc.

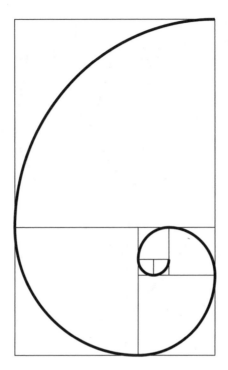

This is called the Fibonacci spiral. A similar curve to this occurs in nature in the shape of a snail shell or some sea shells.

The Fibonacci sequence can also be demonstrated by the Fibonacci tree, which actually occurs in some plants and trees.

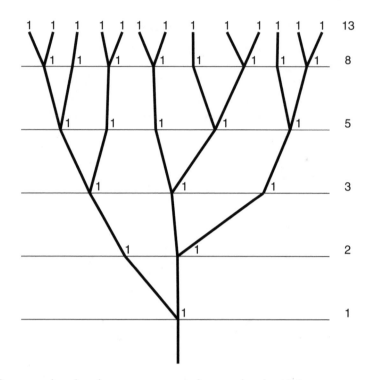

Suppose that the plant grows a new shoot only when it is strong enough to support branching, say after two months. If it then branches every month after that at the growing point, we get the picture shown above.

Nature's use of space

The way nature utilizes space is in many ways closely linked to the Fibonnaci sequence.

Nature is obsessed with patterns. The underlying theme of these patterns is based on mathematics. It occurs over and over again in the way that nature uses number arrangements and space so efficiently.

This can often be seen: spiders have eight legs, pineapples have rows of diamond shaped scales, eight sloping to the left, 13 sloping to the right. In all these cases the numbers mentioned are part of the Fibonacci sequence and the numbers of this sequence occur over and over again in nature.

Other geometric shapes also reveal themselves many times in nature and illustrate the way nature uses these shapes with maximum efficiency.

Bees manufacture their honey in hives that are filled with hexagon shapes, simply because hexagons fit together with no loss of space.

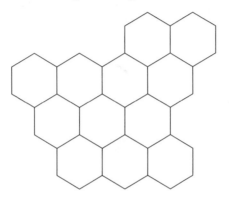

A pentagon, for example, would only fit together with spaces in between, as would circles.

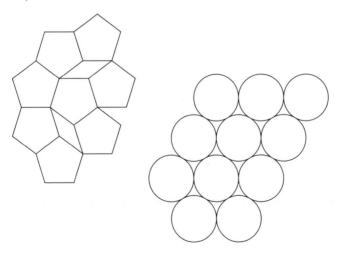

Of all the polygons available, the hexagon is the most economical and strongest for the purpose of a honeycomb.

A snowflake is also always formed in a hexagonal shape. Little is known about these shapes, except that no two snowflakes are exactly the same, and they are formed by vibration. These crystal shapes have a hexagonal symmetry.

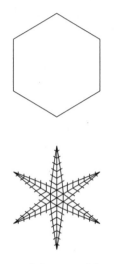

The geometric arrangement of the crystal is caused by surface tension and its molecules. The changes in temperature and humidity form the different shapes, but always in hexagonal form.

On many plants the number of petals is a Fibonacci number, for example buttercups have five petals, an iris has three, some delphiniums have eight, the corn marigold has 13, an aster has 21, pyrethum have 34 and daisies have 34, 55 or even 89.

Fibonacci numbers can also be seen in the arrangements of seeds on flowerheads. Page 167 shows a magnified view of a large sunflower or daisy. The seeds appear to form spirals curving both to the left and to the right of the centre, which is marked with a black dot. If you count those spiralling to the right at the edge of the diagram there are 34, and if you count those spiralling the other way there are 21, two neighbouring numbers in the Fibonacci series.

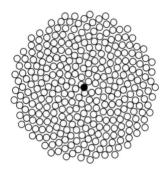

The reason for this is that such an arrangement forms an optimal packing of the seeds so that, irrespective of the size of the seedhead, the individual seeds are uniformly packed, all the seeds are the same size, there is no crowding in the centre and not too few around the edges.

Many plants also reveal Fibonacci numbers in the arrangement of leaves around their stems. If you inspect the arrangement below you will see that Fibonacci numbers occur when counting both the number of times we travel around the stem, going from leaf to leaf, as well as counting the number of leaves we pass before finding a leaf directly above the starting one. In the illustration shown, it is necessary to make three clockwise rotations before we find a leaf directly above the first, passing five leaves on the way. If, however, you travel anti-clockwise it is only necessary to make two rotations, the numbers 2, 3 and 5 being, of course, consecutive Fibonacci numbers.

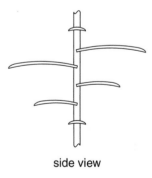

side view   view from top

This is no coincidence, but yet another example of the economical and efficient use nature makes of space. By spacing the leaves precisely in the way it does, nature ensures that each leaf gets a good share of the sunlight and catches the most rain to channel down to its roots.

Appendix 2

Pi

Now I know a rhyme excelling,
In hidden words and magic spelling.
Wranglers perhaps deploring,
For me its nonsense isn't boring.

Pi is the Greek letter (π) used in mathematics as the symbol for the ratio of the circumference of a circle to its diameter. The value of pi is approximately 22/7, or, more accurately 3.141 59; in fact, the above verse is a mnemonic for remembering pi to 20 decimal places, the number of letters in each word coinciding with the digits of pi: 3.141 592 653 589 793 238 46.

The formula for the area of a circle is πr^2, r being the circle's radius. During Biblical times and later, various approximations of the numerical value of the ratio were used; in the Bible it was simply taken to have a value of three, while the Greek mathematician Archimedes correctly estimated the value as being between $3\frac{10}{70}$ and 3i.

The ratio is actually an irrational number, thus the number of decimal places continues to infinity, without any pattern emerging. With modern computers the value has already been taken to more than 100 million decimal places, although this exercise is purely recreational and has no other practical value.

The symbol used to denote pi (π) was first used in 1706 by the English mathematician William Jones (1675–1749), but only became popular after being adopted by the Swiss mathematician Leonhard Euler in 1737.

Appendix 3

Topology and the Mobius strip

A mathematician confided
That a Mobius band is one-sided,
And you'll get quite a laugh,
If you cut one in half,
For it stays in one piece when divided.

Topology, a term coined in the 1930s, deals with those properties of geometric figures that remain unaltered when the space they inhabit is bent, twisted, stretched or deformed in any way.

All cylinders, cones, polyhedra and other simple closed surfaces are topologically equivalent to a sphere, while a closed surface such as a torus (doughnut shape) is not equivalent to a sphere, since no amount of bending or stretching will turn it into one.

One of the foremost pioneers in the field of topology and the properties of one-sided surfaces was the 19th-century German mathematician and astronomer August Ferdinand Mobius.

Mobius was born on 17 November 1790 in Schulpforta, Saxony, and died on 26 September 1868 in Leipzig, Germany. His mother was a descendant of Martin Luther.

His family wanted him to study law, but preferring to follow his own instincts he took up the study of mathematics, astronomy and physics at the University of Leipzig in 1809.

In 1813 Mobius travelled to Gottingen, where he studied astronomy under Karl Friedrich Gauss, considered to be the greatest mathematician of his day, who was also the director of the observatory in Gottingen. Later, Mobius moved to Halle, where he studied under Johann Pfaff, Gauss's teacher.

Although Mobius did publish many important works on astronomy, his most famous works are in mathematics.

Almost all his work was published in Crelle's journal, the first journal devoted exclusively to publishing mathematics. His 1827 work *Der barycentrische Calkud*, on analytical geometry, introduced a configuration now called a Mobius net, which was to play an important role in the development of projective geometry.

Although Mobius gave his name to several important mathematical objects such as the Mobius function, introduced in 1831, and the Mobius inversion formula, the area in which he is most remembered as a pioneer is topology. In a memoir to the Academie des Sciences he discussed the properties of one-sided surfaces, including the Mobius strip, which he had discovered in 1858 as he worked on a question of geometric theory of polyhedra.

Although Mobius was not the first person to discover the curious surface named after him, and now known as a Mobius strip or Mobius band, he was the first person to write extensively on its properties.

It is very easy to construct your own Mobius strip. Start with a long rectangular piece of paper, give the rectangle a half twist of 180° and join the ends together so that A is matched with D and B is matched with C.

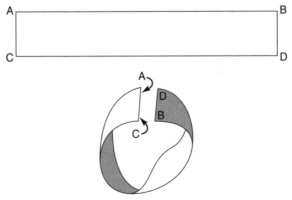

Give the rectangle a half twist.

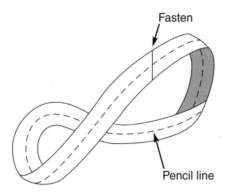

Mobius strips have found a number of applications that exploit the property of one-sidedness that they possess. Joining A to C and B to D would produce a simple belt shaped loop with two sides and two edges and it would be impossible to travel from one side to the other without crossing an edge. With the result of the half-twist, however, the Mobius strip thus created has but one side and one edge.

In order to demonstrate this take a pencil and start anywhere on the surface of the strip and draw a line down its centre. You will find that when your pencil makes it back to where it started you will have covered the whole strip, both *sides* of it, without ever having lifted the pencil off the paper.

Next take a pair of scissors and cut the Mobius strip along the centre line that you have just drawn. The result will be one large loop.

Next, again cut around the centre of the band that you have left after the initial cut. The result this time will be two separate loops, but interlinked with each other.

Giant Mobius strips have been used as conveyor belts that last longer as each *side* gets the same amount of wear, and as continuous-loop recording tapes in order to double the playing time. In the 1960s Sandia Laboratories used Mobius strips in the design of versatile electronic resistors. In the sport of acrobatic skiing, free-style skiers have named one of their more spectacular stunts the Mobius flip.

The Mobius strip has also been interpreted by several artists. The American sculptor Jose de Rivera (1904–85) who is best known for his large metal constructions, created modernist works, such as *Flight* (1938, Newark Museum, New Jersey), that were simplified, stylized constructions of highly polished metal, often variations on the Mobius strip.

The artist M. C. Esher, who used mathematical themes in much of his work, created a famous drawing of ants parading continuously around the strip's one surface. This is perhaps the most famous and recognizable interpretation of the Mobius strip by any artist.